From Grand Dames to stars of po
two decades British actresses ha
enormous media and public atten
rich and varied interviews that ma
sixteen of our best known and loved actresses – up and
coming as well as old hands – candidly reveal the truth about
the pleasures and the slog that make up the mystique and
reality of being an actress.

Carole Woddis has long been involved in the theatre as a
writer, publicist and administrator, and is co-author of *The
Bloomsbury Theatre Guide*. She lives in London.

'SHEER BLOODY MAGIC'

Conversations with Actresses

Edited by
Carole Woddis

To Dorice, my mother, who also once had her eyes set
on the stars

Published by VIRAGO PRESS Limited 1991
20–23 Mandela Street, Camden Town, London NW1 0HQ

This collection and introduction copyright © Carole Woddis 1991

The right of Carole Woddis to be identified as editor of this work
has been asserted by her in accordance with the Copyright, Designs
and Patents Act 1988

A CIP catalogue record for this book is available from the British Library

Typeset by Goodfellow & Egan Ltd., Cambridge
Printed in Great Britain by Cox & Wyman Ltd, Reading, Berkshire

CONTENTS

ACKNOWLEDGEMENTS

I would like to thank a number of people without whose help and support this book would not have been possible.

To Mary Toomey, Judy Scott, and Julia Bryce-Jones for transcribing; to the several theatre PRs who enabled me to catch a number of salient performances, especially Lynne Kirwin, Ann Mair and Mary Fulton; to agents who provided information and fielded infinite numbers of phone calls; to the Theatre Museum for research facilities; to the unfailingly courteous Ian Herbert of *London Theatre Record* for answers to innumerable points of detail.

To the following for enlightening conversations and frequently soothing noises: Sally Robson, Stacey Charlesworth, Gill Spraggs, Fiona Farley, Lyn Gardner, Barney Bardsley, Julia Pascal, Vera Lustig, Helen Mackintosh, Yvonne Brewster, Jules Wright, Robyn Archer, Val Wilmer, Deborah Phillips, Maggie Copeck, Helen Ramsbottom, Ags Irwin, Lily Cornford, Eve Cunningham and all the sisters at no. 61, Fran Willard, Annie Fursland, Caroline Keely, Amanda Theunissen.

Thanks also to Lynnea Toltz for access to her country hideaway; to the women's workspace in Cornwall, Brisons Veor; to Trevor R. Griffiths for his invaluable back-up, to Rosie Martin, Annie Lloyd, Ros Asquith, John Fordham, Sue Sanders and Jeane Nadeau for their many acts of friendship.

Thanks are due particularly, too, to Becky Swift and Ruthie Petrie at Virago for their constant words of encouragement and infinite patience; to my brother and sister-in-law, Paul and Helena Woddis and my dear friend Jessica

Higgs, whose unwavering faith also helped guide the book to its final stages.

Last, but not least, thanks to all those actresses who gave me their time and a little bit of themselves. Without their generosity, there would have been no book at all.

INTRODUCTION

I can remember, as a young girl, leafing through the pages of *Picture Show* and film annuals, prey to an inexhaustible array of unobtainable images that did little for my own self-esteem. Foolish girl! More often than not, I ended feeling broken-hearted, ill at ease with myself. My image of myself never, ever, matched up to those fantastic and fabricated images.

Later, I grew wiser. And I learned, after my heart skipped a beat seeing the young Vanessa Redgrave as Rosalind to Ian Bannen's Orlando in *As You Like It* in the early sixties, that here, in the theatre, was an entrée to a whole new world – and with it a whole new set of images and feelings that would, I realized, lead me to a greater understanding of myself and the world around me. These were images of recognition.

Over the years, I have grown more and more curious about the construction of these images of ourselves as women that so invade our everyday lives – in books, magazines, film, television – above all, for me, in the live experience of theatre.

Theatre really has been the guiding star by which I have endeavoured to find my way. Within its generous forum, I have located a thousand-and-one aspects of myself – not always comfortable, often challenging but ultimately life-enhancing. It is then, as some sort of homage to the women who perform what is, in my eyes, an act of superb daring, that to some extent this book is dedicated.

It is also a search for some answers – to what makes up the image of ourselves as women.

To me, these actresses stand as modern totems – something we imbue with extra properties, apart from ourselves. But, at the same time, they are, distinctly, part of us, ordinary mortals like ourselves.

What do we see in those women who dare to put themselves, as so many refer to it, 'on the line', to create that image that can so easily be shattered by criticism? And, by the same token, why do *they* do it?

To capture the words of some of our foremost actresses might be interesting enough on one level. But, having spent many years of my life working in and writing about the theatre, I wanted to see if something more could be exposed – something truer to the pressures I know go on behind the aura and mystique, and that women, I believe, are so much more susceptible to, given a working world in which the power balance is so often not in their favour.

Cutting through that aura to the human being beneath has proved to be a startling, unpredictable process and has brought me up sharp, if ever I needed confirmation, with just how mysterious a business it is being an actress – mysterious and many hued. There is no one pathway to success. But what do we mean by success? It is such a transient, unpredictable thing, at the best of times, and particularly so in the arts and entertainment world where ideas and images are largely shaped by what is often considered the fashion of the moment.

As Linda Bassett, a favourite actress of mine, has put it: 'To be a popular success, it's not just about the quality of your acting. It's whether you're in tune in some way with what people's fantasies are, what their needs are. I might be telling my truth, but if my truth isn't useful to nine hundred people that night, then they're not gonna get it. I might be giving a wonderful performance, it might be built in fire and blood but if I haven't connected with anything in them, they'll just go "oh yeah".'

So mysteries remain. So, too, the instinctive and understandable desire for self-preservation. As much as actresses are in the business of revealing themselves *on stage*, off-stage, they remain, contrary to public mythology, deeply protective of their own privacy and mechanisms – a fact which also, to some extent, reflects the power nexus that controls their fates.

But how to choose sixteen actresses out of the wealth of talent currently available in this country? A cursory glance produced a list of at least seventy, each one, in her own way, having a different story to tell. Both Virago and I agreed that it would be good to try to reflect as wide a range as possible of background, age and experience, within the context of actresses who were publicly well known.

In the end, selection was dictated partly by personal choice and partly by a process of self-selection. Some didn't want to be interviewed – several of the younger actresses, for example, whom I would have liked to have included. Several were too busy. Some were impossible to pin down with schedules that precluded any notion of 'the odd hour' for interview – it took a year to gain time with Judi Dench, for instance, and then it only came about by a stroke of misfortune that confined her to the house for a number of weeks and which allowed me to go and visit her.

Vanessa Redgrave was away filming during the whole period of composition of the book. So, too, Maggie Smith who was on Broadway.

Then again, while most actresses acknowledge they have to do their share of publicity interviews for a specific role in the next play, film or series, some do not like to talk in general about the business of acting.

Researching and working on this book confirmed one

thing: talking about acting and doing the business itself are two entirely different things. There lurks a certain superstition about putting that process into words, as though something of the magic will be lost in the speaking of it. We, the public, on the other hand, seem to have an insatiable curiosity to know more about these people. Thus, the opposing dynamics of this book: revelation on the one hand, self-protection on the other.

Over the years, actresses acquire self-protective mechanisms that come into operation as soon as you start to talk about acting. Immediately, fears arise about how those words on the page are going to be interpreted. It is a question of image and also one of power relationships. Unless an actress starts her own company, she is not mistress of her own fate. Power is invested in the public and critics who judge the performance, but even more importantly, in the directors, producers and casting directors in whose hands rest the life-and-death casting decisions. And, although it may sound simplistic to say so, acting cannot be done on its own; by its very nature, it requires an audience, witnesses. You are not an actress if you are not performing to someone. Then, what of the image? To reach the pinnacle of success, an actress has to go through, every day of her working life, a myriad number of pressures of censure. As a woman, she must not only match up to some ephemeral idea of 'being good at her job'. For her there is the over-riding pressure of appearance and age. An actress's career is more cruelly subject to the inexorable march of time in the way a male actor's is not – and with that comes a commensurate restriction and choice of work.

Then again, there is the old bogey: is she actually 'good-looking' enough? Does she, in essence, subscribe to certain received ideas a casting director, director or producer may have in his mind (and even if it is a 'she' mind, that mind is as conditioned as the next man's by the dictates of, not to put too fine a point on it, the patriarchal society in which we are all bred) of how this particular female character should 'look'. How, as the actress Ann Mitchell said to me, does she subscribe to some collective notion of the archetypal mother/daughter/spinster? And how is she to endow that character with a humanity that transcends an archetype which can so easily spill over into stereotype? Imbuing women with individuality and showing their diversity is what feminism in acting to some degree, has been all about; that and trying to bring the experience of being a woman three-dimensionally on to the stage or into the studio. For some actresses, righting the imbalance of what they perceive to be continuing stereotypes becomes a driving force in their lives. Equally, what seems to be paramount to many actresses – and certainly the ones I spoke to – is the idea of being faithful to a text: finding the truth of a character within the context of the words written by the playwright, is as applicable to a classical text as it is to a new one. The male gaze, however, in these circumstances, is immensely powerful – albeit, increasingly benevolent. Any actress, no matter how successful, takes a risk when she challenges the power of that status quo from her own standpoint. Some directors, of course, are more sensitive than others to taking ideas from their actors. And as many interviews bear witness, the right to challenge directors has greatly improved over the past decade or so. But there is still a long way to go and, needless to say, this power nexus resides still to some extent, in a status quo of silence.

This book then tries to look into what it means to be an actress in this day and age, where she came from, some of the pressures that might have been upon her in her growing up: what makes her tick as a person; where acting stands in her daily life; what it gives her; what it doesn't give her. And, of course, what some of the roles have meant to her.

In reading the interviews, it is as well to realize that they were conducted through a question and answer process. The questions have, of course, been taken out. What is left, I hope, provides a thought-provoking glimpse into a world that continues to enthral both performer and receiver alike – and that poses as many questions as perhaps it attempts to answer.

The reason why each actress was chosen will, I think, become evident on reading the introduction to each interview. For example, Eileen Atkins is an actress whose work, never less than compelling, seemed to reach some sort of apogee with her portrayal last year of Virginia Woolf. The quality and range of Judi Dench's work, has, over the years, given me so many different pleasures, from her Juliet onwards. Janet Suzman's Cleopatra was, for me, a highlight and her intellectual and political stature seems to grow with every year.

I wanted, by contrast, two actresses from a younger generation whose classical work had already made an impact: thus, Fiona Shaw, interviewed at the National during her run of *The Good Person of Sichuan*, and Harriet Walter.

I also wanted some actresses who would give a different cultural perspective. I had much admired Carmen Munroe in *The Amen Corner* and *A Raisin in the Sun* and as probably the most respected black actress of her generation, I wanted to include her story.

Maureen Lipman has seemed to me one of the truly multi-talented comic actresses of our time; so too, Prunella Scales, who will hate me – as will they all – for labelling her in this fashion.

Jane Lapotaire's vivid personality and unforgettable performances as Piaf and Madame Curie demanded her entry, as did Julia McKenzie, not only for her undisputed musical prowess but also for her undervalued dramatic depths, the range of which, I believe, we have by no means yet seen.

Sue Johnston's work in *Brookside* has been outstanding, by any standards (she was interviewed just before she left the series), and Pam St Clement from the rival *EastEnders* as well as being a public favourite, has a story that needs to be told and has the bravery to let it here be set down.

Julie Christie, too, has been remarkably candid about her own journey through films. And, at the far end of the age range, I wanted Beryl Reid to give a flavour of other times and traditions.

For a younger viewpoint, Cathy Tyson seemed to me to be an actress of enormous potential after her film debut in *Mona Lisa*; Meera Syal, too, whose views represented yet another strand again of the younger generation.

My thanks to them all for their bounteous co-operation and assistance.

Carole Woddis, London

JANE LAPOTAIRE

'What are you – an actor or a mother?'

Born in Suffolk. Trained Bristol Old Vic Theatre School.

Her extraordinary portrayal of Edith Piaf in Pam Gems's *Piaf* shot Jane Lapotaire into the limelight, winning her numerous Best Actress awards – Society of West End, *Plays & Players*, Variety Club of Great Britain – and took her to Broadway (where she won a Tony). Before this, she had served a solid apprenticeship with four years as a member of Olivier's National Theatre Company at the Old Vic.

Her TV appearances as the leading woman counsel in *Blind Justice* (for which she won the Broadcasting Press Guild Best Actress award) and as Madame Curie in *Marie Curie* (BAFTA nomination and Emmy for Best Actress in 1977), in their own way, made just as strong an impact as *Piaf*. An actress of unmistakable definition – she does indeed appear to bring a singular energy on stage – she returned to the National Theatre, appearing in Peter Gill's *Kick for Touch*, Thomas Otway's *Venice Preserved* (with Ian McKellen) and in *Antigone*.

In 1989/90, she scored another triumph when she played American scholar Joy Davidman to Nigel Hawthorne's C.S. Lewis in *Shadowlands* by William Nicholson. She has also starred in the West End musical *Dear Anyone* by Jack Rosenthal, played Shaw's Saint Joan for Anthony Quayle's Compass Company; appeared in Shaw's *Misalliance* and Arthur Miller's *The Archbishop's Ceiling* for the Royal Shakespeare Company and flexed her bilingual muscles with the French actor Jean-Pierre Cassel in *L'Aide Mémoire* at the French Institute in London. In 1990 she played Simone Weil, the French philosopher and mystic in Channel 4's documentary about her.

Films include: *To Catch a King*, Nicolas Roeg's *Eureka* and *Performance*, *Antony and Cleopatra* and Trevor Nunn's *Lady Jane*.

Author of a bestselling autobiography, *Grace and Favour*, she lives with her son in south London.

I was born at the end of 1944. I was illegitimate. My mother was a French orphan who was living in England at that time, as a foster child, with an old lady in Suffolk. I, in turn, was fostered by my mother's foster mother.

I grew up in a very working-class environment, poor working class to a large extent. 'Gran' – my foster mother – was a rough diamond but she was wonderful, cantankerous towards the end, but she lived to nearly ninety-six. She was the one constant giver of security, stability and love – the nearest thing I got to unconditional love.

I don't think I would have described my childhood as happy although I can't say I was unhappy; I would say I was terribly confused. I didn't know who I was or where I belonged or to *whom* I belonged, and it took me a *long* time to work out that I belonged to myself. That didn't come until my early thirties.

My only source of entertainment was the wireless, as for most kids in the fifties – unless you came from a very middle-class family – and it became synonymous for me with escape into a fantasy world. The Methodist church was my sole social outlet. The only times I was allowed out was to church on Sunday morning and Sunday School in the afternoon. Later on, in my teenage years, that was extended to Friday and Saturday night Methodist youth club where I first became involved with drama and dis-covered it was fun getting away from myself.

When I was in the sixth form, I became seriously involved with a production of *Toad of Toad Hall* when I was given the part of Toad. But I wasn't allowed to play it because I got German measles and no amount of persuad-ing would convince my foster mother that the spots wouldn't show under the green makeup. I thought my theatre career was going to be very short-lived.

The following year, we amalgamated with the boys'

grammar school next door and did a production of *Romeo and Juliet* in which I played the part of Juliet. By then, I was *sunk*, hook, line and sinker. I couldn't believe why people said Shakespeare was difficult. 'The orchard walls are high and hard to climb', says Juliet, and I thought, 'Well, that makes perfect sense. What's difficult about that?' I had been mocked mercilessly about Shakespeare the year before. I must have been fourteen or fifteen. We had come to London on a school outing to see Edith Evans and Harry Andrews in *Henry VIII* and I sobbed in the scene where he throws Catherine of Aragon out. I didn't know why I cried, but it obviously hit a nerve and all I remember, as the bus drew away from the theatre, was the thought, 'I'm going to be up there some day. I want to do that'. This, I realized later, boiled down to the fact that if I didn't have the two people in my life who were supposed to love me, i.e., a mother and a father, I was going to have six hundred people who didn't know me, love me. It was as corny and as clichéd as that.

By the time I was doing Juliet, much to my headmistress's disgust, I was also ironing costumes and running errands down at the Ipswich Rep. I'd really got the bug badly by then and wanted to go to drama school after I finished my A levels. I saw there was a lot of love and demonstrative affection backstage at the Rep. The actors were, as I now realize, very open and intimate with each other in a social way. My fella is a barrister and he was *horrified* at the amount of touching that goes on. I had to say to him, 'You mustn't read into this what it would be in your profession. No, I haven't had an affair with that man. We worked together in Bristol twenty years ago and I'm just pleased to see him.' If you play Gene Hackman's wife in a film and, on the first day of shooting, you've got to get into bed with him – not for a sex scene but just for what we call 'an Ovaltine scene' – it's no good standing on your barriers. You've got to break those down and behave like you're this man's wife.

Acting was also a way of getting out of Ipswich. By the time I was a teenager, I did realize that there was a world outside 85 Levington Road. I didn't want to get married and have children and be buried in Ipswich like the rest of the girls I'd been brought up with. I wanted out. Even at twelve, I remember knowing that grammar school held the key to something different, to a better life. I couldn't have articulated it, but I sensed a lot more chances were going to be available to me than, sadly, the girls I'd grown up with.

It's often made me ponder. Is that spark, that determination to go for the 'other', something one is born with, or is it just an instinctive reaction that your life *has* to be elsewhere because where you are is not right?

I knew middle-class girls at the grammar school where I was and used to go home with some of them for tea. Their mothers and fathers would sit and talk about Beethoven or the kids would share what books they'd read together. This was a world I knew *nothing* about.

I devoured literature from a very early age. That, too, was an escape into another world. The local library was my one sanctuary. I didn't realize it then but what I was doing was developing a love of language and a knowledge of sentence structure. To my eternal surprise and that of the rest of the staff at my grammar school, I got a Grade One English A level and Scholarship level, even though I was working at Ipswich Rep and doing Juliet in my spare time.

I applied to and was accepted by Bristol Old Vic School where I trained for two years. (I'd applied to several drama schools, failed to get into RADA and nearly driven Gran mad with my despair.)

I was very lucky. At the end of my training, I was one of

the two students that were chosen to go into the Bristol Old Vic company and did two years there. A lot of one's luck is built on another person's misfortune. The juvenile lead at the Bristol Old Vic became ill, so I was promoted from being acting assistant stage manager (ASM) with five lines, to being juvenile lead by the end of the two years. Somebody from the National Theatre saw me working at Bristol and asked me to audition for Sir Laurence Olivier. I got into the National and spent four years there.

So the whole of my first six years beginning in the business was spent without a day out of work in the classical theatre, watching and working with people like Gielgud, Scofield, Olivier, Joan Plowright, Maggie Smith and Robert Stephens. It was just the most *wonderful* opportunity. Those were the days when, in the true sense of the actor-manager that he was, if you did your ten lines well, Larry gave you twenty-five lines; then he gave you fifty-five lines. There was a real sense of continuity and development because most of us, like Edward Petherbridge, Charlie Kay and Derek Jacobi, were all Larry's 'babies'. We'd been, I presume, 'spotted', in a sense, in various provincial theatres and taken into the company. Sadly, that sense of continuity no longer exists. Present financial strictures mean that actors are employed for each play – although, to a certain extent, it does still exist a bit in the RSC because, if you go to Stratford, it's concomitant with coming into London for a year. So you know you have those two years with the RSC.

A lot of young actors now are horrified by that. In my day, there weren't the openings in television that there are now. You were either a theatre actor or a television actor. These youngsters leave drama school now and get snapped up by the television companies because they're a new face. They see themselves billed as starring in the *Radio Times* or *TV Times* and do four or five years in sitcoms. Then they want to go into the theatre and realize they can't talk or walk and don't know how to handle a classical text.

So I was very lucky. I'm one of the privileged, state-subsidized theatre brats who's been used to the repertoire system – which is why being in the West End is an absolute killer. Your *whole* life becomes the show and, often, I crawl home and I say to my family, 'it's *not* the repetition of the play that gets me down, it's not even so much the routine and habit of going into the same building, at the same time and saying the same lines, although that *is* difficult because it's a contradiction, to my mind, of what theatre's about. What is tough is having a thousand people *staring* at you, night after night, while you *dig* into your soul and display it for all the world to see.'

The nicest thing Peter Brook ever said about actors is that they were probably the most generous people on this planet because they gave of themselves. You don't play a violin as an actor. You play *you*, *your* feelings, *your* understanding of the human predicament.

Very early on, I realized that it was only in theatre that I wasn't going to get typecast as being foreign. I had dark hair, a big nose and a French name. If I was going to get any work in film or television, it would be as Spanish au pairs or foreign women. You see, the purse strings in film and television are still largely held by men and men make the major choices. If men write the scripts, they write them for women who they think are attractive – 20- to 30-year-olds.

That is changing now. There are a few more women producers and scriptwriters and directors. But I've been in the business for twenty-five years and, in all that time, I have only worked with three women directors. Whether women make a difference in those positions, of course, depends. If you're a Margaret Thatcher, then you won't improve the situation for women because you'll go, 'Well, sod you, I got here under my own steam, why can't you?'

If you're an aware woman, as a producer, you will be looking for parts where the leading woman *is* over forty and where you insist that she doesn't get out of bed on camera looking like something from *Dynasty* in full makeup and lip gloss as though straight from the hairdresser's. It's very difficult to break those stereotyped ideas: if you're on camera, as a woman, you've gotta look good! Such rubbish! Thank God for Sissy Spacek and Meryl Streep and Glenda Jackson, who *did* break that chocolate-box image in the seventies. But now I *despair* when I see people like Madonna. It's as if feminism never happened. There's my son with pictures on his wall of this woman who is dressed in what one can only describe as bondage and suspender belts and you think, '*Jeeezus*, what did we *fight* for for over twenty years? *Plus ça change*'. The only comfort about Madonna is that she's in charge of her own empire. She's not being exploited.

Superficially, it would seem that we do have more equality in the theatre than women do in other professions. But it's only surface, because if you are what is called a 'strong' actress, you will often find that you're the only woman in the cast, and that you're dealing with a male director and male stage management. It's often difficult to say, 'Listen, this is my experience as a woman, we're talking about the interpretation of my role and, excuse me, I am the woman and you're all men.' There aren't any hard and fast rules. You just have to feel your way.

I would never be involved in any part that I felt maligned women or put them down or corroborated the stereotype. Obviously, like all actors, I have to do crap every now and again to pay the bills, but I would never actively be involved in anything that I felt was wrong. My feminism is very important to me because of my love of women and the support we have given each other.

The only difference between now and twenty-five years ago is that I don't do every job that comes my way just because I need the exposure. I try only to do the jobs that I think are life-enhancing and life-enriching to the people who watch them; plays with good heart, good soul that I can believe in. But the roles get very thin on the ground between forty and fifty-five for the same reason again. The purse strings are held by men, who want stereotypically attractive women. Thank God, there are a few more women writers now and male writers are now more aware, so you do get the occasional things like *Blind Justice* where the leading woman was over forty – she had to be because she had to be an experienced barrister. But between forty and fifty-five, this is my old adage, you're too old to be the leading lady, but not old enough to be the leading lady's mother. And it is extraordinary, you know. Overnight, from always being the baby in a theatre company, it seemed to me as if somebody had flicked a light switch and *wallop*, I was suddenly the oldest in the cast.

If we were in France and Italy, we wouldn't have the problem because 'les femmes d'une certaine âge' are very much in demand. Women between forty and fifty are considered to be attractive, mature and able to contribute to society. Not in England. Here they like their girls pretty and young and blonde – English roses. I'm being very general and swingeing here but I think it's basically because of the public-school system. Those boys are shunted off to public schools when they're eight. That's the end, to all intents and purposes, of their emotional life and growth. These boys grow up into men who are actually still boys and they're frightened by women who are self-contained, independent, strong and assertive.

9

I think the reason I play 'strong' women is because, oddly enough, I'm not strong at all. In fact, playing 'strong' women allows me to exercise muscles that are often unused in my personal life. People often think I'm stronger than I am. I'm riddled with insecurities and vulnerabilities and I think, 'Oh God, how do I tell the director that actually the situation he's put me in in this scene is wrong?' But I'm able to fight more for the character I'm playing than I can for myself. I manage to manufacture a veneer of being capable and able to cope. Someone once said to me that the best mixture of all is to be strong and vulnerable because a lot of strong women don't have vulnerability. Then again, one mustn't always think that because a director is a woman, she's going to be any more compassionate or understanding. There's no guarantee of that, sadly.

It's my generation of women whose mothers (not in my case but in most cases) grew up expecting nothing more than to marry and have children and, suddenly, here we were, educated and believing we had a right to go to university and all the rest of it as well. We said, actually, we want both. We want families and jobs.

Now, of course, the younger generation take a lot of what we fought for, for granted. The thing I find sad is that a lot of the younger generation of actors haven't got kids. There came a point when I was the only one in my circle of friends who had a child.

I can only say that being a mother has enriched my acting 100 per cent and, if I could have my life again, it would be the first thing I wouldn't change. I love being a mum.

It is very easy, as a female actor, to say, 'Right, I'm dedicated to my career, I'm a feminist, I'm not going to have children'. And it *is* easier, in a way. It is very tough, having children and working, as it is in any profession. One doesn't *ever* want to say to a director, 'Excuse me, could you let me have the afternoon off, it's my son's sports day', as I did once. I was met with, 'Well, you've got to make up your mind. What are you? An actor or a mother?' I said, 'I'm both, actually.' But I didn't go.

Then again, that has to be seen in the light of the nature of the work we do. We must be one of the few professions where people don't take a week off the minute there's the first sign of flu. You think of all these old ladies who've come to the theatre from miles away, on their one outing of the week, or the month, or the year, to find an understudy on. You can't do that. The discipline in the profession is very strong, amongst older actors, at least.

I brought my son up in a very old-fashioned way: 'Eat up, shut up, hurry up and don't talk when grown-ups are talking'. When Rowan was five, I had to take him with me while I was dubbing a film and I said to him, 'You sit in that corner, and don't rustle your drawing book because, if you do, hundreds of pounds' worth of tape are thrown away and I'll only have to do it again. When it's bedtime, you go without mucking about because I have to learn my lines. If I don't learn my lines, I won't do this job well and the director won't employ me again.'

So, from a very early age, he learned that work is about disciplining yourself and it's a serious thing. You don't muck about with it. But I was also determined that no child of mine would ever go a day without knowing that he was loved and wanted, which is something I never knew. Since the day my son was born, I've always put being a mum as a higher priority than my jobs. My attitude to my career fell into what I think is a much healthier sense of proportion because, if a job was offered, the decision about taking it was conditioned by whether I could take Rowan with me. Will Rowan like it? Will he be comfortable? OK, he will, then let's do the job.

I took him all round the world. When he was thirteen, we worked out he'd been to fifteen different countries. He lived with me in New York for a year while I did *Piaf* because I'd realized by that time it didn't matter where we lived as long as I was with him at the end of his day. In fact, we lived in five different homes in three years when my marriage broke up and he was far less unsettled by it than I was, because he knew that Mum was there. He's far more centred as a person at sixteen than I was at thirty-two. I say to him he's the best job I ever did.

But it's exhausting. When a child is small, from the minute you open your eyes to the minute you go to bed, you're at full stretch. You're having to wash, cook, clean, take the child to nursery school, fit in the shopping in the lunch hour – cook, wash, tidy up when you get home.

Of course, there have been what other people call 'sacrifices'. I don't see them as sacrifices. I have turned down work. I have turned down lots of money abroad because, when Rowan was nine, he and I had a long discussion about whether he wanted to go into secondary school in America which would mean staying there from age eleven to eighteen. He decided he wanted to come back to England. My American agent went ape-shit and said, 'You've just waved goodbye to an American career', and I said, 'Well, you know, I'm a mum. He wants to go home to England and I miss my friends and I'm a classical actress and there's really no outlet for a classical actress in New York'. So we came home and I bought my very first house, at thirty-eight, and settled happily into it to provide him with some sort of stability.

Of course, there are problems and they always happen at the worst time. The au pair decides she wants to leave the night before your first night or the first day of your shooting. Or she's got flu and she can't pick him up from school. The time it's most tough is when your kid is ill and you can't be at home. I've had Rowan in my dressing room before now, with me saying, 'I'll make you up a bed here and at least I can see you and I can give you the medicine every three hours'.

It was made slightly more difficult because I didn't have family backup. There wasn't a granny or grandad on either side so it was very lonely and scary. The biggest problem in being a 'single parent' coming from the kind of background that I came from was that I had no role model. Every decision I made about Rowan I made in complete isolation. I didn't have another adult to whom I could say, 'Do you think I've been too hard on him? Am I right? Am I wrong?' The only thing that got me through those years were my women friends.

The blissful day arrived three years ago when we could finally wave goodbye to the last au pair. He can cook for himself and he doesn't need a baby-sitter any more. I can now go away filming for a week or ten days, which is the maximum I allow myself to be away from home during term time, and he'll have a friend come and live-in and they look after themselves and each other. So it's easier for me.

I'm not the kind of actor who goes home and *yearns* to play a part. I get on with the rest of my life when I'm at home. I suppose I would have liked to have had a go at Hamlet in a workshop situation, just to explore a massive text. Most of the leading classical actors in this country will have had a chance to play Hamlet, Henry V, Lear, Richard III, the Scottish play, etc. The biggest female role in Shakespeare is Rosalind.

When I played *Piaf*, the thing that was most crucifying about the part (apart from the terror of singing) was that I had no experience of being the *motor* of a play. Take something like Cleopatra, for example. Cleopatra doesn't come into her own until Act V when Antony is dead. With *Piaf*, I had to drive the play. I was the heart and engine of it. It was a killer to be on stage for two and a half hours, driving fourteen other people. As a woman in the classical theatre, one just doesn't have enough experience of that.

I couldn't exactly use the word 'enjoy' about *Piaf*. I didn't do one performance in three years without feeling terror – and I mean *terror*. It was like starting a boulder rolling. More often than not, I was in front of the boulder and it was rolling after me rather than me being behind the boulder and controlling it. I went down to nearly seven stone.

When it finished on Broadway, the American producer said, 'You know, we could re-edit this and make it into a one-woman show. You could be a millionaire. We could take you around the States to all the university campuses.' I said, 'You must be kidding. I'm an actor, I want to move on. I want to play other parts.'

But I'm grateful for the part. It put me on the map, gave me 'focus'. I used to say little prayers to her spirit and ask her to forgive me if I'd made any wrong value judgements. I think you have an extra obligation when you play somebody who really lived. I read and researched. I looked at every photograph of her and every song she ever sang, every book that was written about her in French and English. You have to explore every avenue just to make sure that you're not making wrong value judgements about this person. Your job is to do the play and to present the person in as truthful, open and honest a way as you can. That's what the pivot of theatre is – presenting human nature to people.

Blind Justice was a real one-off, too – a female lead where the woman was the protagonist, where the woman made things happen. It was interesting, too, because half the press related to that character in exactly the same way as half the crew did. Half of them, who were feminists and sensitive to

14

women, thought she was a wonderful, outspoken, very free character, but several journalists and many of the crew said to me, 'What's it like playing such a ball-breaker?' It's very interesting. The minute a woman becomes assertive, or says 'No, I don't like that, no, I don't agree', she's a ball-breaker. We even had it on *Woman's Hour*. It was the first 'Twenty Questions' type programme that I'd done – with Diane Abbott and Teresa Gorman who, of course, being politicians, have facts at their fingertips and are used to public speaking.

An issue arose where we were questioned about what Margaret Thatcher had done for women. Teresa Gorman, in response to our replies, said, 'Isn't it terrible the way that when women get together they bitch about other women who are successful?' And I said, 'Isn't it odd that when women analyse another woman's character, like Margaret Thatcher, we're accused of bitching, but when men do it, it's called character-analysis.' So even among women who are aware, there is still this terrible kind of stereotyped reaction. Yes, women do have competitive feelings towards other women. I think I did have them when I was younger. But feminism helped us accept and like who *we* were, and put an end to envying *other* women.

When I went into the business, actors belonged to the Garrick Club, did the *Daily Telegraph* crossword, didn't knock over the furniture, and went home. When I was a young actor at the National Theatre, you didn't speak to Maggie Smith, or Geraldine McEwan or Joan Plowright in the wings even when, as in my case, you played Geraldine McEwan's sidekick for nearly four years, unless you were spoken to first.

Then in the sixties, there was a huge influx into the theatre of university-educated actors who said, 'Excuse me, just because you're the director doesn't mean you're always right. I've got a degree in English Literature and I query what you're suggesting we do.' Productions became much more of a corporate effort.

When we did *Piaf*, most of the cast had only been out of drama school two or three years but, because it was directed in such a way that *all* the company were there, involved *all* the time, every day in rehearsal, I'd have these youngsters saying, 'Here, you know that bit where you're supposed to be angry in that scene, well it's not coming over as that'. Half of me would think, 'Well, sod you, I'm up on the stage for two and a half hours, you've only got five minutes of your role.' But the other half of me would think, 'Thank God, they're taking that kind of interest in the production.' That's how much things have changed, just in my working experience.

When I worked with Peter Brook in the late sixties, nobody stood up to him. He sat on a chair, we sat on the floor and we did what he told us. We were terrified and terrorized by him. Jump cut. Fifteen years later when I'm doing *Piaf* at Stratford, they're rehearsing *Antony and Cleopatra* and I meet half the cast wandering up the street in the middle of the day and I say, 'God, this is unheard of'. In my day, if Peter Brook directed a production, you were all there, all the time. You had no choice. One of the young actors said, 'Oh, commitment's extra, love. He's got to prove to us that his production is worth our being there every day when we've only got ten lines to do.' See the difference just in fifteen years! Whether it produces better theatre, I don't know, but at least actors are less regimented and consequently the potential for input based on choice is greater.

I can remember one occasion, rehearsing with Elijah Moshinsky – who is one of those very rare directors who creates an atmosphere in which the actor can make a fool of herself without feeling embarrassed about it – when he said about my character, 'Oh, you should be late for the wedding, Jane, when you get to the registrar's office scene'. I said, 'Wait a minute, she wouldn't be late. She's not that kind of woman, she's organized and efficient. *He* would be late.' And Elijah said, 'Oh yes, much better idea.' Twenty years ago, I wouldn't have had the courage to say that. The director's word was God.

Nobody knows what the right way of doing a play is. Rehearsals are all about exploring the wrong ways because you only find what the right avenue is by a process of elimination. Acting is a very spiritual job, in the best sense. The actor is the medium through which the play travels and you have to get your ego out of the way of that.

I have a friend who has a double first from Oxford who's an actor. She takes directors head on and says, 'What do you mean by that?' She doesn't work much because she's labelled 'a troublemaker'. All she actually does is say what she thinks based on an intelligent assessment. It can be more difficult to get work if you speak out, challenge the director. Mind you, I have noticed that there is an element among the generation younger than me of 'if it's male, let's attack it'. That's no solution, either.

I think one has to identify with what one acts. I feel passionately that, for want of a better word, one acts with the 'feminine' side of one's personality. This is true of men as well. You work with what Jung called the *anima* which is to do with integrity, intuition, myth, magic, mystery – all those things that aren't measurable. The business world and the rational world runs off logic, rationale, all those things that for want of a better word we call 'male', which is why, in the business, most actors tend to be feminine, and I don't mean by that that they're homosexual. I mean they have a greater understanding of their own sensitivity and poetry, if you like, than, let's say, a man who's a banker or a solicitor.

Because the business is so tough, most women have also had to develop their male side. You've got to be able to cope with disappointment. You can't cry because the producer said you've got the job and now the director says he doesn't want you, he wants someone fifteen years younger and prettier and blonde and all the rest of it. I remember a teacher at drama school saying you've got to have the sensitivity of a butterfly and the hide of an elephant. That's exactly it, because it's the sensitivity that you work with and the hide that allows you to survive the let-downs and the heartbreak of the profession.

The other thing is that, inasmuch as one can analyse it – and of course, for every incident I give you, there will be an exception – women actors tend to work very subjectively. They filter their role in the play through whatever experience they've had in their own personal lives. A lot of male actors tend to be mimics. There's a whole legacy within the male tradition of mimicry and imitation. Twenty years ago, there was a tape going round the National Theatre by one of the younger leading actors doing a whole conversation on Waterloo Bridge between Gielgud, Richardson and Olivier. It was brilliant. You couldn't find a female counterpart to that. When have you ever seen a female actor doing a Peggy Ashcroft? You couldn't, she's inimitable. *We* have no tradition – each of us *is* the tradition. Each of us has to carve her own way. I think it's something to do with the journey towards finding out who you are as a woman and what you believe in. It's so fraught with difficulties because of stereotyped attitudes to women: you shouldn't really be there, you should be at home looking after your kids. Every step you take is so tough that the last thing you want to do is throw away the little bit of self-knowledge that you've found and mimic somebody else. It is so difficult for women to get anywhere. Male parts outnumber the female eight to one.

One part I loved playing was Eleanor of Aquitaine in a BBC series called *The Devil's Crown*, not because of the *role* – the series was indifferently directed and inadequately written – but because of the woman. She was the most extraordinarily powerful character. She ruled this country for ten years while Richard Lionheart was at the Crusades. Imprisoned for fifteen years, she kept in touch with politics and literature, and rode to Spain on horseback to get Richard a wife when she was over seventy. She was born in an area of France where my mother's family come from so I felt a special affinity with Poitiers and the area round there. But it was the woman who intrigued me. There's a wonderful story there, of this independent and cultured female (the part played by Katharine Hepburn in *Lion in Winter*). Why no woman writer has ever written a play about her, I don't know.

I used to apologize in my early years when people asked me what job I did. I used to wish I could say I was a nurse or a social worker or a teacher. I wished I could do something that was more overtly of use to society. Then I thought, 'Stop being such a wanker. If you've been given this to do, do it to the best of your ability.' So what's what I try and do. That's why rehearsals are such a strain, because all your pores are open for everything to travel through. That's why you're very sensitive in a rehearsal period.

The word vocation has only just come back into my life. Somebody said that to me recently and I said, 'Yes, you're right, it's a word I've avoided but it is'. And that's why now I really only try, if I can financially, to do work that my soul is behind as well as my heart and my head.

JULIE CHRISTIE

'I'm glad I was part of the sixties'

Born in India. Trained at Central School of Speech and Drama.

Leading icon for a generation of filmgoers, Julie Christie's credits – *Billy Liar*, *Darling*, *Far from the Madding Crowd* (all directed by John Schlesinger), *Dr Zhivago* (director David Lean) and *The Go-Between* (director Joseph Losey) – amount to a check-list of the major British films of the sixties.

During the seventies and eighties, she continued to make films that spanned a variety of themes from Hollywood mainstream – Robert Altman's *McCabe and Mrs Miller*, Nicolas Roeg's dark Venice-based thriller based on the Daphne du Maurier novel, *Don't Look Now* with Donald Sutherland, the Warren Beatty comedies, *Shampoo* and *Heaven Can Wait* – to the experimental and avant-garde: the bleak futurist fantasy, *Memoirs of a Survivor* based on the novel by Doris Lessing, *Return of the Soldier*, about a shell-shocked WWI returnee (with Alan Bates, Ann-Margret, Glenda Jackson), *Gold* directed by Sally Potter, *Heat and Dust*, the historical drama set in India (with Greta Scacchi, Christopher Cazenove and Shashi Kapoor), and *Miss Mary* directed by Maria Luisa Bemberg.

Her most recent film was Pat O'Connor's *Fools of Fortune*, based on the William Trevor novel, set in Ireland in the 1920s.

She now lives in Wales and visits London frequently. She is a campaigner for Third World and environmental issues.

I don't know where wanting to act came from. My mother told me that I said I wanted to act when I was in India, where I was born, which I find quite odd because I can't imagine a lot of theatres in the jungle in Assam. I think I loved showing off.

I was only in India for five years, then I was sent home. My parents came over with me and then went back. It was awful, awful, really bad. I can't remember much about it, I blanked it all out. They left me with a wonderful foster mother, so it was easy to blank out that separation.

I never thought of myself ever going into films. I was always very snobbish about it and when you think about women in British films in the 1960s, there was nothing really to emulate. Women didn't have an active role in films and I was interested in acting. I was interested in theatre and in the classics. I certainly wasn't interested in films. That was *way* down there – vulgar stuff. However, a very good agent called Philip Pearman came to our final show when I was at the Central School of Speech and Drama. Philip obviously saw a pretty face and thought 'we can do something with that'. I think I was probably the first person in my class on any books despite the fact that what I did was of no merit at all. Everybody was terribly envious of me. In fact I remember someone saying, the day after the performance, 'Oh, Philip Pearman's on the phone for you', and it was such a big deal that I thought they were playing a practical joke.

Philip sent me up for an awful lot of films – most of which I didn't get. Then I was sent up for *Billy Liar* and I failed that, too. But the person that had been chosen fell ill and I was given the part. *That* was the turning point. I know it was my looks. I was so bad, it couldn't possibly have been anything else! I just didn't know what I was doing.

I don't know about being the right face at the right time. You'd have to ask other people, because you never think of yourself like that, do you? I know it certainly wasn't because I was so brilliantly talented, so it must have been something else. I thought, 'They don't know. They've made a dreadful mistake. But I won't tell them yet until they find out.' I felt I was terribly, terribly lucky. I really wanted to go into the theatre but I thought if I was going to get into cinema at all, it had to be the respectable side of it, the 'new wave'. That's the only thing that was good enough. Everybody who was anybody in cinema in the sixties wanted to be in the 'kitchen-sink new wave' then – not just me. Getting in to that film was a dream come true, though it's not really as though I really *achieved* anything because it *happened* to me. It was just luck, pure luck.

I got marvellous reviews for *Billy Liar*, absolutely wonderful, as if something really special had just arrived on the screen. I don't quite see what they were going on about but there's a sort of energy and life that for one reason or another excited people. And John Schlesinger, the director, was a very talented man.

I can't remember the exact sequence of events – I went into rep straight after drama school, then did some television, then *Billy Liar*, then Birmingham rep, and somewhere in there was *Doctor Zhivago*, and the RSC after Birmingham. I just recall that after that I started being busy in films. I obviously wasn't wanting to do theatre for some reason. Maybe I became afraid of it. I went back and did *Uncle Vanya* later and found out I was right – I was much better equipped for cinema than theatre. It's to do with presence, for one thing, which I lack on stage, and have on film.

I don't think the characters I played when I was younger were sex objects, though people certainly often refer to them as such.

In *Billy Liar*, I was one of Billy's girlfriends. In retrospect, she was rather emancipated because she goes off on her own and makes Billy an offer: 'You want to come with me?' He says no, so she goes off without him. And he's the loser. Bathsheba in *Far from the Madding Crowd* isn't driven by sexual impulse. She just happens to have three boyfriends!

What drives her is a need to control her own destiny in a world where women aren't expected to do so. So she has to do it through men. But I like doing love stories anyway, because the greatest emotions always go on around that subject and sex.

If anything, I think I've been cast more as romantic. I think the 'sexy' tag is because I made *Darling* and that's what people connect me with. Surprisingly, they only ever connect me with one film. In Britain, it's *Darling*; in America, it's *Dr Zhivago*. They don't connect me with the sixties. *Darling* was an art film in America. Also, it was only a British film whereas *Dr Zhivago* was the sort of film they could relate to in America.

I can't remember much about *Darling*. I just remember feeling terribly tired because of having such a lot of work to do. I think I must have been burning the candle at both ends. I was in almost every shot so I remember half the time just falling asleep on the floor at the end of the shot. I was very bad-tempered and very tired. It was another one of those things that in retrospect people say all sorts of things about – the part being some sort of departure for a woman, to be organizing and choosing her own life. That may well be true. I think it did do something different from the others, but it was also a very moralistic tale. She had to pay for not being a good girl, getting married, settling down and having children. *Darling* didn't strike me as being particularly trend-setting, because it was just a part. A really good part.

But I wasn't just an actress doing a job. I was a *young* actress being looked at as an object all over the place, having photographers running around after me, *endless* interviews, seeing myself all over the place in magazines – all of them objectifying me. It would be very hard for any of that not to penetrate into the subconscious – though it wasn't until years later that I realized the cumulative effect of all this. I didn't go with all the hoo-haa. I always rather looked down on the whole process; I think I must have been born a bit of a snob! It wasn't acting I thought was silly. I think acting and films are wonderful. It's all the rubbish around it, the personalization and the marketing. I distrust marketing of any sort and I really don't like advertising and that's all that you are, on the whole, when you're being interviewed, photographed, put into magazines and talked about – an advertisement. You're being used as an advertising tool for somebody to make a lot of money out of. In British films, it's different, of course. The sums of money involved are infinitesimal compared with North American films.

I talk about being 'put' into magazines. But of course, I collude in that. Nowadays, the majority won't go and see or buy or do anything unless it has some personality cult attached to it. On the whole, unless people have read an article about someone connected with it, they won't turn out to see a film.

I'm glad I was part of the sixties. I think the values were great. We were rejecting consumerism and trying to discover the spiritual values – and also hedonistic values. Hedonism was very strong, after the hypocritical fifties. People were actually trying to refute the power of the multinationals which are driving us in the West into more and more consumption and, consequently, the Third World into more and more poverty. We did it by cutting down on our own consumption. It was chic to have less, not more, in those days.

I know people associate me with the Kings Road but I don't know why. I did live not far from the Kings Road. But I was more down the Portobello Road. That was my hangout in those days. I wore hardly any makeup, I still don't. Black eyeliner, very pale lipstick and that was about it. Gobs of mascara. And lots of second-hand clothes. That again was to do with recycling and nonconsumerism. It's sad to see young people nowadays buying designer clothes and feeling that's what they have to do because they're driven into it by advertising and the market.

Even being older, I'm lucky enough to have an almost permanent choice of scripts. Perhaps I haven't had as wide a range as some people but I don't know whether I was up to doing a wider range. Maybe I'll widen it now as my ability grows. I've always been quite rigorous in my choices, but I know more now. In the old days, I might have quite happily made an adventure film in an Arab country with a whole load of Arabs running around acting like stereotyped Arabs because I wouldn't have known what that implies in terms of world power and that it's a ploy. Now, I wouldn't do it, and that's a real nuisance if it's a damn good story and the woman's part is good.

Maybe it is unusual to let politics determine your choice, not just ours, in any line of business. I don't think it *is* politics with me, it's morality. Everybody has a different code. If I think something's wrong, I don't want to be connected with it. It could be called escapism because I'm not actually doing anything to help anybody, I'm simply removing myself. It is, in fact, quite a selfish thing. It would be important if everybody did it. If we all refused to act in the hundreds of racist, sexist, sadistic and plain dishonest films that are made, then it would be important. Impossible though, if you don't have the cash to support your morality.

I've never really felt typecast because such a lot was always going on with the women I played. Of course, things are different as you get older. This year I got offered two very good women's parts, one of which I'm doing. They're uncompromising, they're people of my age, they live a full, whole life and they're the centre of attention. But the fact that I'm amazed to get offered even *two* of that quality perhaps indicates something. There are just fewer good parts for women of my age. I've only got to look around at our society to see what it means to reach middle age and how it is devalued. So it's going to be devalued in my job as well. I couldn't expect anything else. It's up to us to build the value of it up, really.

There's nothing I burningly want to play. I did play Masha in *Three Sisters* on the radio and I really enjoyed that very much but I'm too old to do it off the radio. Perhaps those classical parts would be the most rewarding, perhaps not. Life's too short. I don't want to put myself through the agony of learning all those lines! So it depends absolutely on what comes through the door. I'm a completely passive recipient!

I wouldn't say I've done comedy yet. That's something I want to do. *Shampoo* was a comedy but I didn't play it as one. The comedy was all from a man's point of view. And when I talk about comedy, I think being a woman is such a ridiculous and funny thing sometimes that that's the sort of comedy I'd like to do – the stuff that nobody ever, ever, puts into films. I don't actually like working with the camera very much. I'm just beginning to learn to like it more now. Instinctively, I turn my head away from the camera. Ask any lighting camera operator and they'll tell you.

I enjoy making films because of the life they bring with them. That usually means the country as well because you're often in a wonderful place that you'd never otherwise go to. I'm always interested in the history, so there's a whole new area of knowledge that starts to build up, that makes its own world. And you meet people in that place, you make new friends, not necessarily in the film. *Fools of Fortune* was different. We were a very small, close unit. And oh, Ireland, delicious Ireland. I'd say I made a couple of close friends on that which is quite unusual.

I always used to bring my friends out for work because I felt so privileged to be going abroad all the time and living in the sort of beautiful accommodation you can get (rented houses, I hate hotels). My greatest pleasure is to have my friends over and share this marvellous thing. Afterwards, I remember the experience and the place where a particular film is made, I don't remember much about the work.

I remember a lot about *Fools of Fortune* because I had decided I couldn't blunder along in the dark any more and that I should start taking acting lessons. So now I have a marvellous acting teacher. I started to learn the job, if you like. So the actual work on that film will remain in my head because for the first time I knew what I was doing. For the past twenty-five years, I've been winging it. No wonder I'm a nervous wreck! Acting has meant absolute terror to me. But now that I've got this acting teacher, she makes it all a wonderful discovery, journey and adventure.

I relied a lot on directors. I kept doing it thinking all the time that I was going to give up being an actress, I didn't like being so vulnerable. But I didn't know anything else I could do. I did think of all sorts of jobs but I'm not equipped to do anything else. It's true – what a thing to find out! I'd like to work more with women directors. I loved working with Sally Potter in *Gold* and Maria Bemberg in *Miss Mary*. There's a given – things are understood and many things are shared through common experience. It's very different. Obviously, there's a lack of paternalism although paternalism has been very useful to me in the past. By the time I'd started working with women, I'd learned about that. I'd already decided to do something about me and paternalism. So it was a great pleasure to be working on more equal terms.

The struggle to get things off the ground for a woman director in this country is heartbreaking. I have immense respect for those who are hanging in there despite all the rebuffs. Today, I was at a meeting where somebody was talking about bursaries for new directors and they read out all the directors and every single one was a man again and I thought, 'Where are the women in this? There aren't any'. Why are there so few women directors? I don't know. They're not there so it's not even a question of choice, whether to work with them or not.

I'm not an organizer or a businesswoman at all. I'm not the sort of person who's ambitious for control of her own company. In a way, I wish I was, because it would be nice to be in control of films and really be able to create them for myself.

I think I've been terribly privileged. I've had the best of everything. I don't know why. I'm very fussy about trusting people. Perhaps I've got a good detection system for searching out insincerity and dishonesty. But who knows?

I've only ever made one film in Hollywood – *Shampoo*. I don't recall much of it, but I seem to remember it being a somewhat lifeless experience. Los Angeles is OK. It's a cinema town and almost all my friends there were in the cinema, whereas in Britain I don't have any friends in the cinema. London certainly isn't a cinema town. LA is like a steel town and being in the steel business you're going to have a lot of friends in it. I like people in my profession very much. We all know the same job. We all know what we're going through.

People get very few offers over here now because there's not as much being made. Our film industry is in great danger. There's much less on offer now than when I started and that's because we've been consistently underfunded.

Funding has just gone down and down. It's like British Rail, it has to have state support to function properly.

Whether I'm working in Los Angeles or Argentina everybody seems to be eminently competent and doing the job very well. The big difference is in this *huge* question of money. In Argentina, you have to wait while they do something with the camera because they actually haven't got the equipment. They don't have that camera there or you have to shoot on that take because they haven't got any more film. And, let's face it, there's the difference of the money in your own pocket.

Miss Mary, the Argentine film I made, opened here but didn't get much notice because we have distributors who don't give a toss about anything except big American films. Small-budget films like that – it was a lovely, dreamy film about the English governess of a wealthy Argentine family – don't get distributed in the provinces. They only distribute things like *Aliens*, or gang and science-fiction films, or films about war and violence. I guess the majority of distributors probably don't know anything about cinema or care about it. They just care about the profits. Making a film is like Truffaut's *Day for Night* – that's how I always think of it. We're all doing a different job – actors, hairdressers, carpenters. We're all in different worlds in a way, yet we're in the same world and all shoved together and having to live together and enjoying each other. It lasts no time at all. Then you get objectified.

People have always made fantasies about something, I suppose, but sometimes people behave to me as if I'm not real! They clearly don't think I am. They almost poke me – 'Oh, look, it's Julie Christie'. It's so funny. In America it's particularly pronounced. I used to think cinema was a religion for Americans but it's changing and now I think it's TV soap stars who have become their religious icons.

PRUNELLA SCALES

'Quite pretty enough for all normal purposes'

Born in Surrey. Trained at the Old Vic Theatre School and with Uta Hagen, New York.

A much loved actress, Prunella Scales is inextricably associated in the public mind with Sybil Fawlty, long-suffering wife to John Cleese's Basil Fawlty in the BBC's *Fawlty Towers*; the creator, too, of Sarah in the BBC's *After Henry* series and Lucia in London Weekend Television's *Mapp and Lucia*, adapted from the E.F. Benson novel.

In a long theatre career, she's taken leading roles in new plays by Michael Frayn (*Make and Break*) and Simon Gray (*Quartermaine's Terms*), played Annie Parker in J.B. Priestley's *When We Are Married* and on the fringe appeared in Joe Orton's *Ruffian on the Stairs* (at the Soho Poly in 1973 with John Hurt and David Warner) and played all six female characters in *Anatol* by Schnitzler at the Open Space. At the National in 1989, her portrayal of the Queen in Alan Bennett's *Single Spies* was a performance of subtle and comic perfection. Also at the Royal National Theatre, she played Mrs Candour in their production of *School for Scandal* and, in 1991, takes on the heroin-addicted wife, Mary, in Eugene O'Neill's American classic *Long Day's Journey*.

As well as television appearances in plays by Alan Bennett, Richard Harris (*Outside Edge*), Alan Ayckbourn (*Absurd Person Singular*) and appearing as Mulie – 'a repellent woman from Leatherhead' – in the BBC's *Beyond the Pale* (adapted from the William Trevor novel), she has directed at Bristol Old Vic, Cambridge Arts, Nottingham Playhouse, Almost Free (London), and National Theatre of West Australia.

Films have included Jack Clayton's *The Lonely Passion of Judith Hearne* with Maggie Smith, and the film version of Alan Ayckbourn's *Chorus of Disapproval*.

She is married to actor Timothy West. They live in London and have two sons.

Both my parents are northerners although I was born in darkest Surrey. Rather unusually for the daughter of a Yorkshire merchant – I think nowadays you would say import–export person – my mother was an actress before she married. My grandfather had a warehouse in Bradford. He was musical, interested in literature, as a lot of people were in Bradford which was a very cultural place in the late nineteenth and early twentieth century – Delius concerts, that sort of thing.

My mother was the youngest of four. Her sister went to Bradford Grammar School, and she, because she was the youngest, was sent south to a girls' boarding school which was *highly* progressive for those days. While she was there she decided she wanted to be an actress which was really not something you did at all then in manufacturing circles.

My mother left RADA to look after my grandmother – single-daughter syndrome – and, after her mother's death, she went to Liverpool Rep and worked there for two or three years. Then she came to London where she met my father who was nothing to do with the theatre at all. He was also what you'd call impoverished middle class, I suppose. He'd been axed from the Indian Army after the Great War and worked for a cotton firm.

They married and started up life in the early thirties with very little money. You didn't need very much then but they were always extremely hard up. Certainly there *had* been some money in my mother's family but it seems to have disappeared completely by the time she married. They simply had what my father earned as a salesman; they never owned their own house or their own car. However, they were both extremely interested in the theatre and, from when I was very little, they took me and my brother to art galleries, concerts and plays. They scraped and saved to give us what they thought was a good academic education – the best education they could. I went to the same school as my mother because that's what they loved and believed in. Actually, I got a sort of scholarship.

From the age of about eight I wanted to be an actress. I did a lot of acting at school. The assistant headmistress, a lady called Mona Swann who's still alive, had been on the staff at the Theatre Studio run by Michel Saint-Denis (where Peter Ustinov started) and she was intensely interested in speech and drama.

Michel Saint-Denis, George Devine and Glen Byam Shaw founded the Old Vic Theatre School after the Second World War. Mona said, 'This is the best and most progressive school, Michel Saint-Denis is the best drama teacher in the world and you must audition for that if you want to be an actress.' I auditioned and got in.

I came out of drama school with two ambitions: to work in the classical repertoire, by which I mean European and world repertoire, and to be in new plays. But it's only now that I've *started* to work in classical repertoire. And it's only in the last ten years that I've been playing substantial parts in significant *new* plays either. I've just had a lot of bad luck, I suppose. I think I haven't had very fashionable looks. It's all right now I'm middle-aged, it doesn't matter. When I was younger, it was the elfin, Audrey Hepburn look and I had a face like a bun. I'm afraid appearance is a *bit* important, which is why I think our son, Sam, is likely to do well, if he has a lot of luck. He works very hard, but he's never going to lose a part through not looking good enough, which constantly happened to me. At Salisbury and Oxford, Frank Hauser gave me lots of fascinating parts and found me 'quite pretty enough for all normal purposes' as Thornton Wilder says. I played Nora in *A Doll's House*, Desdemona, all sorts of things. Homages to people like Frank Hauser. Actually, I can't complain. It must be said that I've always been pretty busy, maybe because I'm quite a *useful* actress, quite versatile. But it's always been two steps forward and one step back, throughout my career, and no doubt that will go on until I die.

I think the biggest buzz for an actor is to feel that because of what you do, the audience enjoys the text more. That's why I like working at the National Theatre. I've done a lot of 'non-textual' plays, a hell of a lot of improvisation and stuff like that. I originally wanted to be a dancer (my mother took us to a lot of ballet). Not being a creative person myself, to feel *necessary* to the creative process is a tremendous buzz. The creative people are writers and painters and musicians and composers. I suppose the biggest buzz in the world would be to be a singer or an instrumentalist; I think it must be agony to be a composer or a writer. But if sometimes we can kid ourselves that we are *necessary* to the interpretation of the writer's vision, that's the nearest we come to feeling we *are* instrumentalists or singers.

No! – I don't think my work is important. I wish it were but I'm sure it isn't, although I think *art* is important, desperately important. I think art is crucial. I think actors *can* be important nowadays because of the exposure they get on television. For a short time after that exposure, the public are going to take some notice of what you do, and therefore you have a chance to introduce them to things they might not otherwise meet. There's nothing more moving in the whole world to me than people falling about at a 400-year-old joke – or even a 200-year-old joke. I find that exciting because we are now working in the most *appallingly* philistine atmosphere where no regard or value is placed by our masters on this *priceless* linguistic heritage we have. We have a *huge* responsibility and I mind terribly about being involved in it. That is why it's so satisfying to be working in *School for Scandal*. I've been in the business thirty-five years and never played Sheridan before.

It's not anybody's fault except the *funding*. Nobody can afford to do it now. At the Oxford Playhouse in the fifties, we did Farquhar and Shakespeare and Sartre. Nowadays, the regions can't afford it. Well they do . . . Bristol Old Vic did *Othello* last season, which I saw. It was a *splendid* production; *very* well played; *packed* to the roof – they did 120 per cent business. But Bristol is in deep trouble now, not because they are not filling the theatre but because they can't get the subsidy. I think it's disgusting. Even more so when you think that a company like Prospect went to the wall in 1981 for lack of a sum which was the funding that a regional town in West Germany would have got for half a year, for *one* of their buildings – and, moreover, a regional town with two opera houses and *three* theatres.

In the UK, we pay the lowest amount per capita towards the performing arts of any country in the EEC except Portugal – less than half what they pay in Sweden, Germany, France and Holland – and we are the nation that produced Shakespeare, Congreve, Sheridan, Shaw and Wilde (I know most of those are Irish). We have got the richest dramaturgy in the world, probably in the whole of history apart from the Greeks, and possibly even richer than theirs, and we have a government in power which attaches *so* little importance to it *even commercially* – let alone sociologically, emotionally and psychologically – that we can't afford to do the buggers. There is so much that central government could be doing to put it right. They could remove VAT on theatre seats; they could make local government support of regional theatres mandatory rather than discretionary, like libraries. And they could abolish the ridiculous new tax regulation whereby young actors are taxed at source – PAYE – *on theatre earnings only*, which means directors can't persuade talented young actors to go into theatre at all.

*   *   *

I haven't, on the whole, found the age thing a problem. I mean, I never lie about my age but I don't go on about it a lot because I am still playing forty-year-old parts. On TV, I've been playing Sarah in *After Henry*, quite a long running sitcom. She's supposed to be not a day over forty-two at the beginning of the series, which means I've been playing her years younger than myself and no one's complained. I'm playing Mrs Candour in *School for Scandal* well into her fifties. People were quite surprised, but I just wanted her to have this elderly thing about her.

I simply *hate* the distinction being drawn between comedy acting and any other kind of acting. I think this categorization of styles – and particularly of actors – denies the public the opportunity of seeing some extremely talented performers in different parts, and it denies actors the chance of bringing their various perceptions to different branches of the business. I'm not only talking about comedians playing Hamlet, I'm talking about Hamlets playing sitcom, or whatever.

I hate, too, this 'light entertainment' category that you get in television. There's a 'sitcom' category even within the comedy category and I'm afraid it is to do with money. 'Sitcom' has to have a wide appeal, it has to be fairly bland, it has to be all kinds of things. Satirical comedy can deal with slightly more dodgy things and you put it on a little bit later in the evening and it requires people like John Cleese and Rowan Atkinson to break the moulds.

I have had to deal a lot with 'British comedy writing' and I use the quotes with reluctance because I hate the genre. I mean, I don't hate the genre, I hate the *concept* of the genre. In 'British comedy', if you are a woman, you are not allowed to be funny unless you are post-menopausal or so eccentric as not to be a sexual threat. That has been true for many, many years. Now it is no longer true thanks to the brilliance and efforts and talent of people like Victoria Wood, Emma Thompson and French and Saunders, but it has been a long haul and, not being a creative person, alas, I have done nothing to change that situation myself.

I don't think of Sybil Fawlty as necessarily sexually unacceptable. I thought she was quite smart, and quite attractive in her way, but now, when people meet me in the street, they say: 'Oh, aren't you nice?', in tones of pained surprise, so quite evidently I have created a monster whom nobody would go to bed with if you paid them. I'm very surprised by that. My function in the thing was to be as irritating as possible to Basil – technically speaking, to be a 'feed' to Basil. That's why we decided she should be less posh than he was – we thought it would be a perpetual irritant to him. (She was actually based on somebody I saw when I was seven.)

I don't feel particularly 'lumbered' with Sybil. It certainly didn't do my career any *harm*. People come along now to other things I'm in. There's a programme I do with two very fine musicians called *An Evening with Queen Victoria*. I don't think when people come they imagine they're going to see Sybil Fawlty meets Disraeli. The public are more intelligent than the media and managements give them credit for. If they've enjoyed you in one thing, they're quite intelligent enough to know that it isn't you really. We've been doing *Queen Victoria* for eleven years now and it's nearly always packed, and it's nothing to do with Sybil Fawlty, not remotely.

I do feel, though, that the reason why I haven't played the classics much before is that I've been categorized as a 'comedienne'. There is a tendency in the UK and in modern British writing, except the very finest, to categorize people. There is this sense of being *only* a comedienne, *only* a character actress and there is indeed an idea in most people's minds, that it is in some way less important, less considerable and less worthy of respect than being any other kind of actor.

I really don't think that I am a better or worse comedienne than any other actress you'd like to name. I just can't bear there to be this *category*. Perhaps certain actors have a better sense of timing than other actors, and there are certain actors and actresses who are frightened of what they think of as 'comedy'. They think of it as a special phenomenon. Getting laughs, I suppose, *is* a special skill, but I don't think it's nearly as important as people seem to think it is. It can be learned, and you can improve the skill. I do a class at The Actors' Centre sometimes, called 'How to Get the Laughs with the Words' and there used to be a class at the Old Vic School called 'Comic Technique' where we would examine why something was funny or why it wasn't.

It's really to do with your perception. I think most of the best actors are good comedians. John Gielgud is a *beautiful* comedian, his comic technique is impeccable. So is Paul Scofield's, and so was Olivier's. All the best actors and actresses – Kenneth Branagh, Judi Dench, Dorothy Tutin, Maggie Smith – are brilliant comedians.

Comedy is based on pain but, for some reason, there is a sense in people's minds that, if you can laugh at it, it isn't important. Peter Barnes once wrote a play called *Laughter*, which said if you laugh at something you stop minding about it. It was an extraordinarily brave play about Auschwitz, suggesting that in some way laughter, because it defuses things, stops you caring about them. There may be some truth in that. The play wasn't as successful as it deserved, and I don't think the idea has ever been fully examined.

Playing the Queen in Alan Bennett's *Single Spies* took lots of research. Luckily, she's very well documented! I spent many weeks looking at tapes and pictures and books before the start of rehearsals, and during the rehearsal period. I didn't feel particularly awed by the subject. It was very kind of her not to mind, or not to object. Actually, the writing was not offensive in any way, although the scene was hilariously funny. In fact, it was extremely affectionate and respectful writing – compared with *Spitting Image* it was a miracle of restraint. Finding the right key for playing that character was to do with finding the right sense of style. As Gielgud said, 'A sense of style is knowing what kind of play you're in.' If it worked, then that was to do with the writing. I'm just a person who plays writing, is lucky enough to play some very good writing, particularly latterly. That's all.

I'm not being falsely modest here (we're all fearfully self-centred people, actors, really) but I was trained at the Old Vic School in the absolutely straight, direct, Stanislavski approach: *who* is this person? how do I find out what this person is like? how do I make myself as like this person as possible and then what does the person *do*, to serve the play and the writer? It's your moral artistic duty to do that as thoroughly as possible. God, doesn't that sound pompous?

I think I'm probably a better actress now, a more skilful actress, than when I started, although still, even after thirty years in the business, I don't get any less scared when I go out there. Maybe I'm more assured nowadays and once I'm 'played in', trust myself a little bit more. I was extremely nervous and unconfident in my youth, both as a person and an actress. It does depend on people having faith in you and that's why I come back to Frank Hauser, the parts he trusted me with and how much he taught me about modern European playwrights. I owe him a great deal. I think a number of actors and actresses would say the same. Indeed, you owe anybody who casts you in a nice part a debt, because of the faith they put in you. That's another point. When somebody says, 'What would you like to play next?', I think most of the actors and actresses I know would rather not say. They would rather be *asked* to play a part, because the sort of faith and energy which it takes to cast yourself ought to come from *outside*. It takes too much out of you, quite apart from the actual mounting of the production. Personally, and I am sure this is true of many other actors, I think artistically you need 'taking care of', up to a point. Whether that's just conditioning, or that I'm wrong about that, and that one should have the guts and energy and faith to be able to mount things for oneself, I don't know.

One's own choices, with rare exceptions, tend not to work. I don't know what it is, but I can't help feeling that if I said, 'I would like to play the Countess in *All's Well*, that's a part I've always wanted to play, let's put it on and I will play it', I wouldn't be as good and people wouldn't find me as good in it as if somebody said, 'Look, we're going to do *All's Well*, will you come and play the Countess?' Perhaps I feel it wouldn't be so successful because I'd know and the public would know, that I'd cast myself in the part. I'd be afraid of their thinking, 'Right, baby, you think you can play this part, prove it'.

I did cast myself once, it must be said, as Queen Victoria. Somebody else compiled the programme, but I'd always wanted to do it ever since I'd read her journals. It has been extremely successful and I'm quite good in it. I don't know why I don't feel bad about that. Maybe because it was a co-operative venture – Katrina Hendry made the compilation, her husband Richard Burnett arranged and plays the music, and Ian Partridge sings in it. We care more about the journals themselves than us in the parts. Somehow or other, that seems to have worked, perhaps because it's very small scale and I'm not risking anybody's money. It's a specialized thing and very refreshing to do. You're not really saying,

'Get me in this part'. You're saying, 'What about this very interesting journal?' But it's *very* difficult to deal with, the 'get me in this part' phenomenon.

One of the happiest jobs I have ever done was *When We Were Married* which was a complete team thing at the Whitehall, a most marvellous cast. I did have a jolly nice part and, actually, I did cast myself in that because Ron Eyre said, 'Will you be in it?' and I said, 'Yes, if I can play Annie'. And he said, 'Oh, I hadn't thought of you as an Annie', and I said, 'Well, please, will you?' So in a sense, I *did* cast myself and the rehearsals were absolute agony. It was frightful, but in the end it worked out. I just desperately wanted to play Annie because it wasn't very obvious casting – the meek, down-trodden one, you see – and I was *blissfully* happy eventually, it was perfectly OK. So maybe one should speak up more often about things one wants to play.

I love that company thing – the sort of thing we had in *When We Were Married*. There is a certain kind of selfishness you *should* have, just as there is also a certain kind of *un*selfishness you absolutely *must* have. The ability to shine when necessary but not to the detriment of the production is frightfully important and it shows from the front. There are some actors who are maybe just as skilled as other actors and just as talented or well cast but that generosity is lacking and that is what will make the difference between their perform-ance and another one. Tim, my husband, is a terrific company man, a father to the company sometimes to the neglect of his own part – he'll be generous and unselfish to a fault. I'm usually much too worried about my own part to do that.

There are lots of parts I would have liked to play but never got the chance. More than anything, I'd like to have played Sonya in *Uncle Vanya*. I know all actresses want to play Sonya but it is nearly always the prettiest girl in the cast with her hair scraped back and, until Imelda Staunton played it, I'd never seen it played as *truly* plain as it should be, as bravely plain, as totally sexually unacceptably plain as I believe it should be. It was terrifically appealing.

I would have liked at one time, too, to have played Viola and all the travesty 'breeches' parts. I've played Helena in *All's Well* on disc, in fact a number of parts on the radio and on disc that I'd have loved to play in the theatre. I'd have *loved* to have played Cecily or Gwendolen in *The Importance of Being Ernest*. I did it on radio with Barbara Leigh Hunt as Gwendolen comparatively recently and everybody said, 'Who are those clever young juveniles?' Nobody knew, until they looked it up in the *Radio Times*. I was well able to play it when I was the right age but never got the chance. Perhaps I was hideous-looking. I was also very hard up. I did help my parents a bit, and had to take more or less what came along. Sometimes, it must be said, I did miss chances through not being available. I didn't really start to make progress until I could afford, very late in life when I was already married, actually to say I will *not* necessarily accept the next job, and that was long after the children were born. (After giving birth, you accept anything just to get back to work.) It's only very recently, probably in the last fifteen years, that I've been able to afford the luxury of saying no. Actually, I don't think it's a luxury, it's courage. I didn't have that courage.

I don't think, even if I'd had private means, things would have been any easier, because there's the *psychological* horror of being out of work, too. Then, occasionally, you take a job that you think you want to do, that turns out to be a disaster. It's so much a question of choosing the right thing but, I have to say, I didn't have enormous opportunities. I can't look back on a time when I had a wonderful opportunity which I totally messed up.

I was in the film of *Hobson's Choice* for David Lean when I was very young and he was lovely and very encouraging. He said, 'Now, in your next movie, make sure it's in colour, you look good in colour.' I was sent along to a lot of interviews and never got the parts because of not looking quite good enough. Looks count more in films, I think. As Tim says, we've both got these acres of irrelevant flesh on our faces. It's all right for him, he can grow a beard over it.

I think things are better now because, since the sixties, people don't look for conventional beauty in young actresses any more except for *very* exceptional parts. I think things are looking up like mad for young female actors, and the women's movement has done a great deal for us all in the theatre.

I've never found any particular problem about being a woman as far as directing is concerned. I like directing very much but I've only done about ten professional productions in my life. Judi Dench and Geraldine McEwan have *sailed* into directing, and it's no surprise that they're both very good. They've worked with more directors than most directors have had hot dinners. Most directors have worked as assistants with only one other director in their lives, if that. There are no schools, so they don't know what works and what doesn't. It's a question of trial and error. I wish there were classes for directors and I think directors *should* sit in on many productions and have experience as actors.

I haven't ever gone out of my way to direct, particularly when the children were young. It is incredibly taxing, 24-hours-a-day work. As an actor you go in and rehearse, then have a coffee break and then you may be free to go home and learn your lines. As a director, you direct the first scene, then in the coffee break somebody says, 'Would you look at the programme notes?' You then direct the next scene and, in the lunch hour, you discuss the furniture. You are *always* there, and when you go home, you have to think about it all night.

I hope to direct again, if I'm asked, but I've earned my living as an *actress* and very often accepted jobs as an actress I didn't particularly like, to pay the rent. I would *not* accept a play that I didn't want to direct because, luckily, I don't have to. But perhaps that's really artistic laziness.

I don't particularly like cameras very much either, partly because of this frightful hang-up I have about my face. When I was very young, I thought I wasn't very attractive which I think might have been my mother's doing. She was a bit puritanical and didn't want me to get vain. So I've never thought of the camera particularly as a friend. I'm getting better at it. I've just played quite a big part with Jeremy Irons in *A Chorus of Disapproval*. I learnt a lot about the camera and began to deal with it better, learning to think on camera.

I *hate* doing sitcom in front of the camera. It's like the hovercraft, which combines all the horrors of sailing and flying with none of the pleasures. Sitcom on television carries all the horrors of weekly rep without the advantage of seven performances, where you've learned something from the audiences by the second house on Saturday. On camera, you only do it once and it's *torture*. I would much, much, much rather do sitcom in the theatre. There are certain *plays* I would rather do on camera but a situation comedy I'd always rather do in the theatre where you have the live audience on *that* night, and they are the people you have to please at *that* time, and the next night you can repair your mistakes. You have a chance to improve. Where there are comic points to be made, you learn to make them better. But I hate eight shows a week and that's why it's lovely being in repertoire. Chichester has a repertoire system and so had the Old Vic. They've always been the happiest times of my life.

I did *love When We Were Married* at the Whitehall Theatre

but, even there, I could have done without eight performances a week, particularly as our dressing room was up
sixty-two stairs and we had to climb them four times every
evening, eight times on matinée days. The room was the size
of this table and I was sharing it with Tim. But it worked
very well, we were very happy. It's true, we were living
together 24-hours-a-day because we were rehearsing a BBC
television play at the same time. We spend more time
together at different times than most conventional couples
where the wife is at home or they have different jobs.

We have two boys – one of twenty-four and one of
twenty-one. The elder one is an actor and the younger one is
still at university. He says he wants to be a teacher and,
although I know teachers are criminally underpaid, I think
we need them so badly I pray he stays with that. He's not
half a bad actor either. But I'd have to say, 'Don't put your
son on the stage.' You couldn't advise your child to do it
because it can be so heartbreaking and there are so many
disappointments.

The good thing is that you never stop. I haven't done
anything *like* all the things I want to do in the theatre yet, but
there's still time. I suppose I'm an optimist. You have to be.
You have to face quite early on that there are some parts you
will never play, but I might *direct* some of the parts I'd have
liked to play.

I directed *Uncle Vanya* recently and the girl who played
Sonya was *wonderful*, partly, I hope, because of my ideas on
it. She was a very good actress anyway, but it was wonderful
to be able to see some of the ideas used that I'd been
thinking about all my life.

I did feel very unlucky for quite a long time and maybe I
was. I could have been a much more useful actress than I was
allowed to be, trolling around in some pretty tatty tours. But
the last fifteen years I've been *incredibly* lucky: *Make and*

Break, Quartermaine's Terms, Single Spies and now *School for Scandal*. Perhaps I'll be more useful now. It's just taken a long time to come to the boil, that's all.

A woman on the bus the other day leant over and tapped me on the shoulder just before she got off and said, 'Saw you on the telly last night, haven't you improved'. Perhaps it's true.

CATHY TYSON

'Miranda, with a Scouse accent?'

Born Kingston-upon-Thames, brought up in Liverpool. Cathy Tyson came to prominence in her first film role playing the young prostitute, Simone, opposite Bob Hoskins in Neil Jordan's *Mona Lisa*, a performance that was universally well received: 'Miss Tyson plays Simone as a girl purged of self-pity, grown old and watchful and unfeeling long before her time' (*Sight and Sound*, August 1986).

A product of Liverpool's Everyman youth theatre where she played Miranda in *The Tempest*, she went straight from there into the Royal Shakespeare Company for their 1984/5 season, and was one of the Golden Girls in Louise Page's play of the same name, about sport and sponsorship.

After a year off looking after her baby son, she returned to the Everyman to play Ophelia in *Hamlet* and the title role in *Educating Rita* at Theatr Clwyd in 1990.

On television, she has appeared in *Scully* and *The Lenny Henry Show*; also *The Practice, Rules of Engagement*, and Central's *Chancer* drama series.

Other films include: *Business as Usual* (with Glenda Jackson), *The Serpent and the Rainbow* and a leading role in *Turbulence*, Adam Kossoff's film on sexual abuse for Channel 4, seen in the London Film Festival in 1990 and due for screening on television in 1991.

She lives in London with her small son.

An actor's career goes through light and shade. If you constantly get film after film, it's fine, but I'd be bored. It's nice not having anything for a while. It's given me a chance to sit back and then try again. I like starting again. I like variety.

My mum had a career in social work and brought me up single-handedly in Liverpool. Now, I'm in the same position myself. I was married for four years and have a child of two called Jack, but I'm not married now. I had all these feelings that I wouldn't be a good mother. It's something you never really know – you have to risk it. Acting is still important to me so I bounce between the two. I think being a mother is very creative.

Getting married and having kids is so taboo with women at the moment; the emphasis is all on their careers. I've felt pressurized by this attitude but I'm feeling more balanced now. It's taken a lot to deal with the baby, but never forgetting about myself, about what I've got planned. My day is very busy. I still want to achieve things as an actress that I haven't achieved yet, and that means keeping fit.

Things have never been easy for me. In rehearsal I get very self-conscious but I'm getting better. I'm learning to be less inhibited, but at first I was terrible. Working in film, where you rehearse in front of everybody and then do it, has helped. Ever since I did a bit of film and my mistakes were seen by all the crew, it's given me more confidence.

I've only been working as an actress for six years. I wouldn't mind doing anything really, just to get more experience. I love working on the stage. I'd like something long, like a contract for six months. I like working with people. That's what I miss. Being an out-of-work actor is a very isolated life. You spend an awful lot of time on your own. So you have to go out daily and throw yourself into what the rest of the world is doing, and not vegetate in the house. I keep reading. I never used to read when I was at school. I didn't have the concentration then. Now I read a lot and enjoy it. When I was leaving school, I read *The Merchant of Venice*. I really identified with some of Shylock's speeches: 'Hath not a Jew eyes, hath not a Jew hands, organs, dimensions . . . if you prick us do we not bleed'. I read that and thought, 'if theatre can identify how I feel . . .'

I left school at sixteen and auditioned at a local technical college where they did an A level drama course. I chose Shylock's speech to audition with. It didn't matter to me that it was a male speech. Then I left college and went to work on a government scheme, taking plays out to the community. We did a lot of acting, physical work, putting plays on, improvising.

It was in college that I first felt I wanted to act. I read *The House of Bernarda Alba* and auditioned for the maid, Poncia. I was having such a laugh doing the play, but I really loved it as well, and whilst I was sitting in the library one day I thought, 'I could actually earn a living at this'. I'd found what I wanted to do. I was seventeen when it dawned on me.

I went to the Everyman Theatre in Liverpool and was picked from the youth theatre to be in two of their shows. Then an agent arranged for an audition with the RSC to play in Louise Page's *Golden Girls*. It was a big shock. I was a wide-eyed, naive kid when I went there and I felt the directors were very patronizing. I was playing Miranda in *The Tempest* at the time and, when I told them this, one of them said, 'Miranda? With a Scouse accent?' I said, 'Well I'm not just doing it in my own back yard, you know, mate. I can do different accents as well.' I thought, what a snob – what a condescending attitude.

I strutted out of there thinking, 'I'll show them, all these men' – there were five or six on the panel: Adrian Noble, Barry Kyle, Ron Daniels, John Caird. Barry was the one who was directing *Golden Girls*, so he was a lot nicer to me. The others were just looking at this weird creature from Liverpool who's black – a very rare species at the RSC at that time! I stood up for myself, walked out of the room and thought, 'Oh, I'll kiss that one goodbye'. But then they turned round and said yes.

I thought they were patronizing in the audition, but at

least we were talking. There was even less contact when we got to Stratford. I think they thought they were the aristocracy and we actors were the paupers. There was an intellectual division between the directors and the actors. We never saw the directors except in rehearsals and, if you weren't doing very much, you weren't talked to basically, just watched. I did five plays altogether: *Golden Girls*; *Love's Labour's Lost*; an understudy in *The Merchant of Venice*; *Red Noses* by Peter Barnes; and *Hamlet*.

I learned a lot of discipline through being on the stage and not talking but having to listen to what everybody else had to say. I had to listen to stay alive, I didn't want to go dead on stage. Luckily, I was listening to something good. It was hard for me to understand the plays so listening helped me to get into them. I never got bored with that and there were some things that never ceased to amaze me. I'd like to do more Shakespeare. I think I've got the potential. I'd like to see the kind of cross-casting that Declan Donnellan has done at the National Theatre – blacks playing whites' fathers and so on. You never know, though, when you're turned down at audition, whether it's to do with your colour or not. They never tell you. It's like any casting: you might be too big, not good-looking, too thin or too fat, not black enough, too black. When I was younger I relished auditions and I want that still to remain in me, but the confidence has gone a bit.

I still am a bit cocky. When I was younger, I would race to an audition and I'd arrive panting with a big smile on my face and just deliver my words. And I got the jobs. A lot of the time it was my positiveness that got me the jobs, regardless of what I could do.

I'm twenty-five. When I was sixteen I thought I could be the greatest actress on earth. But now I realize there's a lot of competition. Luckily, I really thought I was the best thing in the world. It's really important for an actress to believe in herself, without feeling superior. I was cheeky even at school. Cheek has got me a long way. But it's not the same thing as confidence. That's what I've realized this year: I've got a lot of cheek and not much confidence. That sounds like a contradiction, but confidence is a bit more sure of itself and cheek is a bit defensive. Cheek has a shock effect – it's defiant, and I like that. I've still got a lot of that in me. I'm not going to change it but as I'm getting older, I'm getting to know more about how I tick. Acting helps a great deal with that. Even before I acted, I was constantly analysing myself and others. I think a lot, too much perhaps, but I also like to just dance and throw everything away and have a good laugh. I'm Irish-Liverpuddlian-Trinidadian. Trinidadians talk a lot. When my family and all the other Trinidadians around me are in a room, the television is hardly ever on because you know you're going to be entertained with talk out of their mouth.

After *Golden Girls*, I did *Mona Lisa* with Bob Hoskins. I really enjoyed working with Bob and with Neil Jordan. He was very reassuring and transformed me from a very erratic personality on screen. When I did the screen test, he said, 'Your face is all over the place. Put it through the eyes. Narrow it down'. I understood what he meant but doing it for the first time was like being without your limbs.

I had good press in Britain and America. I've always been treated well by the press. I don't go out to get it but they like me. I got a lot of offers after *Mona Lisa*, similar roles but not as good. There was a danger of being stereotyped but that wasn't the thing that bothered me. What I hate is having to be in the position of undermining a proud black woman. I didn't want to demean my race at all, my integrity, by the things they were asking me to do. There was a lot of money involved but something inside me said, 'No'. I've got my boundaries. Going naked: I haven't done that yet. Now I feel confident enough, perhaps I'm pretty near to agreeing to it, but you have to be careful what you do with it.

I have to like my work. I won't do it if it doesn't interest me. So far, I've been lucky in what I've done because most of it has been stimulating work, such as *Educating Rita* at Mold, with Theatr Clwyd and Toby Robertson. He's such a lovely man. The director was Marina Caldarone. It doesn't really matter what sex the director is as long as they're good and she was. She was only twenty-six. We used to have great girlie chats.

I didn't find playing Rita easy. Even though I come from her area, I could not grasp her character. It was a puzzle and I had to work it out. I thought she was thick; I didn't respect her at first. I'd seen the film ages ago and what I saw was a Liverpool girl, a Scouse, that's all. But there's a lot more to her than that. She's got depth and a lot of guts. So has the man. They're a match in a way. He's very good for her because he doesn't completely pity her. She thinks he wants to patronize her and he does to some extent, but there are all sorts of things that she's got wrong about his idea of life as well. They both patronize each other. I think she's a desperate character, desperate to get out of her circumstances and, of course, she does. I'd like to do the play again with more time because we only had three weeks' rehearsal. We did talk an awful lot instead of ploughing through. We had a good time. There were only three of us in the rehearsal room plus the stage manager. Then, suddenly, we had to take it on to the stage, let other people in on it. It was a strange experience for me.

Rita was my first leading role and I don't think I did it well which is why I'd like to go back to it. We only ran it for three weeks. I'd just started to relax in to it and make it my own and then I had to leave it and go away. But I have not had a dull five or six years. I've just been in a film where I played a dancer, and I'd never done that before. It was about a young girl coming to terms with sexual abuse. I played a dancer that the girl meets through her uncle. The dancer talks to her and listens to what she has to say and puts her finger on why the girl has behavioural problems. The film's called *Turbulence*. Adam Kossoff was the director. He's lovely, Adam, very quiet but very funny. It was his first time with a group of actors and everything was very right-on; everything equally shared. There were three actresses and three actors – a really nice atmosphere. Having women on the set meant there weren't so many inhibitions from the women. There might have been from the men. Adam's really shy. But it was as good as you could want it to be.

The next thing is to create that atmosphere in a mixed company. It's very hard to let your inhibitions go when there are more men than women there. When there are more women, I feel I can make a real fool of myself. I felt that with *Golden Girls* where there were lots of women. But I was very young, only eighteen, and I was very respectful of rules and aware of the big RSC crowd, above our heads really. But we had a lot of laughs there, especially in training.

I've got a few things in the pipeline now but they're all a bit vague. I think I'd like to do some singing and definitely dancing, if it's not too late to start. You need to be so strong. I am fairly strong physically. After going through months of rigorous training which was utterly exhausting but really fulfilling, I actually began to enjoy it. I'd only done dancing in discos before but I like dancing and I'd like to combine it with acting. I feel quite excited about that. Maybe something inside's getting out. It's wonderful just to free up. Acting's my main thing, but I would like to go into a different area that I've never done before, risk it a bit.

EILEEN ATKINS

'They're yawning in row F3 & 4'

Born north London, trained at Guildhall School of Music and Drama.

A consummate actress with a long and distinguished career in classical and modern work, both in Britain and in the United States, she was outstanding in the title role of Shaw's *Saint Joan* and also as Hermione Hushabye in his *Heartbreak House*, as Elizabeth I in Robert Bolt's *Vivat! Vivat Regina!*, 'Childie' (opposite Beryl Reid) in Frank Marcus's *The Killing of Sister George* (for which she won the *Evening Standard* Best Actress award in 1965 and made her Broadway debut in 1966), and in Marguerite Duras's *Suzanna Andler*. In 1989, she also won a Best Supporting Actress award for her short but telling impact in Harold Pinter's *Mountain Language*, along with her role as The Queen in *Cymbeline*, both at the Royal National Theatre.

Amongst many leading roles for television some of best and most recent work includes the long-suffering Mrs Morel in the BBC's excellent D.H. Lawrence adaptation of *Sons and Lovers*, *A Better Class of Person* in which she played John Osborne's mother, and the TV drama about television evangelism, *The Vision*, with Lee Remick and Dirk Bogarde.

Last year she starred with Paul Scofield and Alec McCowen in Jeffrey Archer's *Exclusive* in the West End, and later played the lead in Andrew Davies' *Prin* on Broadway. She has just finished the film *Let Him Have It* (about the Bentley/Craig affair), directed by Peter Medak. She is also the co-creator of the blockbusting series, *Upstairs, Downstairs* with actress Jean Marsh; a second, *The House of Elliott*, is due in 1991.

Her portrayal of Virginia Woolf, however, in *A Room of One's Own* (again, seen on both sides of the Atlantic), must be regarded as one of her finest, of which one critic wrote: 'Atkins' sole possession of the stage is unwavering – the prose is near-musical in pacing and assurance . . . her irony, expertly tempered, distils like dew in the theatre, leaving us captivated' (Clive Fisher, *Punch*).

She is married to TV producer Bill Shepherd, and lives in Chiswick, London.

My mother sent me to dancing class when I was three. I screamed, shouted, hated it, told lies to try to get out of it. I was five when the war started. She tried to send me again, then – I think, to try and distract me from the war because I was very frightened of the bombs. She didn't marry until she was thirty-nine and then she had three children. I was born from a terrible row – at least, that's what my father told my first husband, Julian Glover. My mother was forty-six. Of course, she thought I was the most valuable thing in the world. She had always wanted a girl. Mum was a dressmaker and every penny was spent on me. I became an extremely spoilt child of a working-class family. I wasn't actually a pretty child but I was the epitome of what every working-class mother wanted her child to look like then. I had blonde hair that my mother used to curl. I had big blue eyes and I was perky and full of myself, a sort of Shirley Temple lookalike. I used to show off. I was foul, a foul child.

Then suddenly, when I was seven, I became quite plain. I'd also become a very good tap dancer and from seven onwards began to earn money dancing in working-men's clubs. I'd be dancing until half past nine, ten at night, not getting home until eleven. Often I'd fall asleep in school. I had wonderful teachers who tried to explain to my parents that it was very bad for me to be doing all this. But I was getting fifteen bob a go, so if I earned thirty bob a week that made a lot of difference to the family income.

My mum lived to a great age, until she was ninety-four. A very dominant, obstinate woman. I see myself in her every day. She was very fat when I was young. My parents were like a joke postcard. She was huge and my father was frightfully good-looking but short. People used to say, 'This can't be your mother!' Later, when she got diabetes and became thinner, I could see that we were absolutely alike.

My father adored having a girl and told me terrific stories.

He'd been in service but by the time I was born my mother made him give it up; she thought it was degrading. He thought it was wonderful. I got a lot of the stories for *Upstairs Downstairs* from him.

Mother was the one who drove me to dancing class. It was the way out of the working class then. It still is; all entertainment is. That's the only real door open to a repressed class. And education. That's my thing. I can't bear it if people don't put education absolutely top. My father was very worried about me being educated and didn't let me have books in the house. He didn't want me to be educated beyond him because then he would feel silly. I can remember when I started to learn to read – one of the most thrilling moments of my life. It was outside the Regal, Edmonton and I suddenly realized I could put all the words of the Bovril advertisement together. I remember my father looking depressed and me being absolutely thrilled. My mother was rather like the woman I played in D.H. Lawrence's *Sons and Lovers* because she did very much want us all to better ourselves. So I was pushed on all corners – school and dancing.

The woman who was the head of the dancing class I went to tried to adopt me and, when my mother finally said no, she asked if my mother would let her pay for me to go to a little private school. I went to this fabulous private school, two guineas a term in Tottenham, one of the largest mixed grammar schools there were then with over thirteen hundred children. There, I met this bizarre man who changed my whole life. I was just twelve and E. Jimmy Burton was our divinity master. I was mad about religion. The Bible's very dramatic and theatrical and when I read it the two of us thoroughly enjoyed ourselves. The rest of the class hated it.

Mr Burton was also the drama teacher and he cast me as Alice in *Alice in Wonderland* when I was twelve. That did it.

After that I just kept saying to my mother, 'I don't want to dance, I want to do this'. I was wildly happy then, I loved school. Sometimes when I dream, I dream I'm back in school.

I had a very strong cockney accent and my dancing teacher suggested to my mother that I would do better if I spoke well. One day, Jimmy Burton stopped me and said, 'I hear you want to learn to speak decently. I'll teach you for nothing but you've got to come when I say so.' He was a fantastic teacher. I went to see *Dead Poets Society* and it reminded me terribly of him. He was way ahead of Lee Strasberg, and brave enough to do it. I didn't know at the time but I was told afterwards that they always had someone patrolling the room outside to make sure that nothing was going on between him and me. I must say he behaved impeccably.

He was the first person to take me to see a play, *King John* at Regent's Park. After *King John*, I wrote to Robert Atkins, who was running Regent's Park Theatre, saying I'd just played Prince Arthur myself at school: 'Your Prince Arthur is absolutely dreadful. I just played it and I'm much better. Yours. Eileen Atkins.' I had a letter back saying, 'Well, if you think you're so much better come and show me'. I was fifteen. I went to London and remember dressing atrociously in a *Woman's Own* outfit that my mother had made – a dreadful crochet hat, a hideous dress that buttoned down the side, white wedge shoes and white gloves. I thought I looked divine.

When I finally found Robert Atkins and did the famous speech ('must you with hot irons burn out both mine eyes'), he said, 'You're quite right, you're much better than my Prince Arthur. If you want to become an actress, you've got to go to drama school and if at the end of that you come to me and you say you want to be an actress, I'll give you a job.'

I rushed back and told my parents who were appalled because they wanted me out earning money. I was always bottom of the class and, one day, Mr Burton took me to a huge typing pool in Tottenham and said, 'Is this how you want to spend the rest of your life, as a typist?' I was horrified and, by then, I did so want to be an actress. I think it took me a year to pull myself up but I did it and got seven out of eight subjects in matriculation.

Then there was the business of getting into drama school. Mr Burton suggested I try for a scholarship to RADA and also put in for Guildhall for a teaching course because it was easier to get a grant to teach than act. I didn't want to be a teacher, I wanted to be an actress. I tried for the scholarship but didn't get it. Still, I was terribly lucky. I wouldn't be able to do it today because everything is separated now but, in those days, Guildhall was a complete mess, nobody knew where anybody was. I was on the teaching course but I found that if I simply went in there for nine o'clock in the morning and stayed until ten o'clock at night, I could go to all the acting classes and nobody noticed. I don't think I saw the sun for three years.

I got about four prizes and who should come in and do the prizes but Robert Atkins. And he did offer me a job, the perfect one really. I went straight from drama school into playing Jacquenetta in *Love's Labour's Lost* which is a lovely little part, and walk-on and understudy in *Twelfth Night*. But when I finished at Regent's Park, I was pretty well out of work for nine years. I was nineteen. I had no contacts in the world, and it's all done by who you know or you have to be ravishingly pretty. I was walking around trying to get work at the time of the 'New Look' when people were still wearing white gloves. I used to get dreadful little ASM jobs with four months out of work in between. Then I'd come home again for a year.

I didn't have an agent but I used to 'do' the agents, up and down the stairs in Charing Cross Road, knocking on people's doors. One of those terrible people rang me because a girl had gone ill in a Christmas show in Norwich and they needed a replacement very quickly.

I got on a train the night before Christmas Eve and I was met at the station by the most desperate-looking young woman, one kid in her arms, one kid in her hand, who said 'Are you the new girl?' We went through the town and out into the countryside where there was a fairground. Her husband was the man who threw dag-gers round the naked woman inside, which was her, and they'd lost the girl who stood outside in a G-string, doing a bit of singing and dancing to bring people in. That was the job!

Now, I just think it's funny, but there were lots of jobs like that. It's a cruel business. I don't encourage young people to go into it because I reckon if you really want to do it, you'll do it anyway. Nothing stopped me. Inside, I just knew I was an actress. I had no dreams, I never wanted to be famous, I had no desire to be recognized. All I wanted to do was act because that was what made me happy.

I think I'm not as good an actress as I might be because of a slight cowardice. People tell me I'm not cowardly but I think I am, a bit. It was cowardly to get married. I wasn't in love with Julian. On the way to my wedding I called out of the taxi window when I saw somebody I'd been an ASM for in rep – her name was Christine Humphries, I'll always remember. I shouted out, 'Christie, Christie, I'm going to be married, save me!' I knew I was doing the wrong thing but I don't see how I could have kept going without Julian keeping me. I couldn't stay at home any longer, the pressure was so great not to be an actress by then.

I had met Julian at Butlin's. I was walking in Oxford Street one day and as I went past Butlin's, I thought, 'I wonder if I could get into their rep company?' So I wrote off and got into Butlin's in Skegness. Julian had just got out of the Army and he'd got in too. We did three plays a week twice nightly and, at the weekends, because we didn't earn enough money, we washed up in the café.

It seems like another life looking back but if, inside you, all you want to do is act and be with other people with the same passion, it's what you do. When other actors say to me, 'Oh, I can't bear actors like that', I think, 'Well, you must have had a very easy time when you started because unless you eat, sleep and dream it, you can't get through all that'.

After I married Julian, he got a job at Stratford as a spear-carrier and all that mattered to me was that I was going to be around the company. I didn't look like an actress, I still don't. People always think I'm a social worker or a teacher. It wasn't the 'look' then. When I was in my late twenties, Lynn Redgrave and Rita Tushingham were the first two to come in who obviously weren't the blonde little glamorous numbers who were starting to have a career. It's changed now but, until I was twenty-nine, it was pure murder.

Of course, as soon as I started to do well, Julian and I split up. We'd served each other's purposes. We never even quarrelled. He was wonderful, he got me into the company at Stratford as a non-speaking walk-on. I was over the moon. To be in the rehearsal room and watch people like Peggy Ashcroft and Michael Redgrave rehearse was bliss. I thought I was in heaven. I got terribly angry with all the actors for being flippant, I couldn't bear them laughing so much backstage. I thought everyone should be very earnest and talking about 'the work' all the time. I must have been a real pain in the arse.

*　　*　　*

Considering my beginnings, I do now regard myself as successful. All I want to do is go on acting until I drop dead. By middle age, however, you lose ambition, as most people think of it. You have to, because there are no longer the huge parts so there's no point. You've got wherever you're going to get so nothing's going to happen to you now. It doesn't worry me because I love acting. To me the horror would be to have to stop.

I made myself laugh this morning. I'm on television all this week at five to eleven reading poetry. I thought, 'I'll just see what I look like' because I knew that I didn't like the makeup. I was absolutely fascinated. I was right about the makeup. I looked awful. I read not badly and I thought, 'It's funny Eileen, you come across as quite formidable, as if you know an awful lot. Why doesn't the daft side of me come across?' I'm not allowed to do comedy. It's to do with the face.

Years ago, one of the best performances that has stayed in my mind was Geraldine McEwan in *A Flea in Her Ear*, I don't remember her getting an award for it. I think it's outrageous that Prunella Scales, who was simply superb in Alan Bennett's *Single Spies*, is not recognized for the great comic actress she is. Comedy is simply not as highly regarded as tragedy and it is far more difficult to be funny, to make people laugh than cry. That's why you are triumphant when you make people laugh, but I will not put in anything to get a laugh if it's not true. I have to stick to what I think is the writer's intent.

The laugh is the one thing the actor can hear – where you think, 'Ah, we're in touch, we're holding together, it's all right'. Sometimes, in heavy tragedy, you've no idea. Unfortunately, I've got very good, long-distance eyesight and I can see people yawning. The other actors come off thinking they're doing well, and I say, 'No, they're yawning in row F 3 and 4'.

* * *

I really don't think awards are important but I loved reading Richard Eyre in *The Times*. He said he's not really an envious person but there is always a little slither of ice that goes into his heart when he's just made a failure of something and somebody else is being highly praised. I get competitive but only with actors who are in the same age group as myself. In that way, I couldn't be more unfortunate because everybody knows there was an *extraordinary* crop of actresses born between 1930 and 1940. Ten years younger, it's not the same. Right out in front are the four huge ones: Vanessa Redgrave, Glenda Jackson, Maggie Smith and Judi Dench. I happen to *dote* on Judi Dench and Maggie Smith. I think they're both brilliant. The other two, I know, are brilliant and sometimes I like them and sometimes I don't. I still get a twinge, but if they play something brilliantly, I don't want to do it. I just think, 'What's the point, they've done it. It's been done.'

Awards don't necessarily give you more power. All that really matters is what the people who really know think of you. It does matter what Judi Dench thinks of me, or what Richard Eyre and Peter Hall think of me. And they're the ones who are employing. That can mean that sometimes I don't go out to please my audience as some actors do. If they don't like it, hard cheese. I know when I've failed, only too well.

When I was young, I had this feeling when I started a part that inside me there is a steel rod covered in barnacles. As I worked, they would fall off and if that wasn't a shining spear by the time I came to perform, I hadn't got there. Sometimes you can't get the barnacles off because the play isn't well written enough in the first place and there's nothing you can do about that. I've always tried to do good work, or what I consider to be good work, although one of the reasons I did the Jeffrey Archer play, *Exclusive*, was more to do with my mother's obstinacy. When I read it, I thought, 'It's not a great play but it's OK and a lot of people will enjoy it.' But when I started to say to my friends, 'I quite like the Jeffrey Archer play', such shock/horror came over their faces that I was determined to do it. I think people's prejudices are beyond belief! I've got to do what *I* like and if the rest of the world doesn't like it then I'll have to be out of work.

Most of the plays I've done in the theatre have been male authors except for Marguerite Duras; that's why I do her so much, because she writes about women. I've got this strange theory that all the parts that I've most enjoyed playing are when the male author for some reason puts his thoughts and feelings into the female character. In *The Cocktail Party* and *Saint Joan*, there is no doubt that T.S. Eliot thinks as Celia Coplestone; in *Saint Joan*, Shaw has put a lot of himself into Joan, bizarre as that sounds when he's not even a believer. There's a lot of comedy in *Saint Joan* and he's put a lot of himself into that.

With Shakespeare, I infinitely prefer what is known as the 'breeches' parts. I've played Viola three times and Rosalind twice and they are my absolute ace, number one favourite parts. I mostly try not to think about roles I might like to play. Either they're going to come my way or they're not. Hamlet isn't one of them. A woman playing Hamlet is rubbish. How can you find it in you to play a man? Why should anyone want to go and see it except out of some strange curiosity? I think a woman in the same position would be quite different. I'd rather see a schoolboy doing it than a brilliant actress. A schoolboy's rather marvellous acting Shakespeare anyway because of a quality of purity.

Peter Hall rehearses Shakespeare, as far as I am concerned, absolutely the correct way. For many weeks he keeps his eyes on the text and doesn't look at you at all. He's looking to see if you're observing the line endings. That seems to me to be utterly correct because what you're trying to do is to get the truth of what's written on the page, not take it up and arse about with it and show off and think how different you can make it.

I feel much the same about improvisation which was very much the thing in the sixties. People made so much of it. I hate it. There's nothing remotely real about it. Everybody's just trying to score off each other. Funnily enough, it can be really useful if you're working on Shakespeare and you've got someone in the company who is frightened by the language – you do get young kids now who, because they're 'doing Shakespeare', can't be an ordinary person. Sometimes it is terribly good to put it into your own language – I do it myself. But as for imagining what you were like in the womb or going back – sorry, rubbish.

I still find it quite difficult to exert power. But I've noticed in many companies where there's a predominance of male actors – which is more often than not the norm with Shakespeare, nine men to one woman – it's only because I'm an old boot and middle aged that my voice is listened to. A male playing minute parts would be listened to before a young girl playing the lead. It's automatic. You can't even blame them for it. It's what happens, particularly in this country.

I can't help *but* speak out in rehearsals. Sometimes other people get upset and think that there is a row going on between me and the director when there isn't. It's just a fast exchange of ideas without too much politeness. Quite frankly, so often, as a woman, you have to think of the director's balls, to keep saying, 'Oh yes, how wonderful'. I think what comes tremendously into rehearsals is sexuality and attraction of any kind. That doesn't necessarily stop as you get older because you can be in love with someone of ninety – you can be attracted to that personality.

When I was young, I really did think I knew best. I can imagine I was pretty tough to direct sometimes. As I've got older, I've realized almost anybody knows better than I do. I would say, in the last fifteen to twenty years, I've been much more open to direction than I was. I always lap up everything because that's the bit I like. To me, rehearsal is like a huge giant crossword that you've got to fill in and anybody that can help jog your memory or help you reach something can be right. There was a time when a lot of younger actors were very nervous of working with me. When I came to do *Saint Joan*, it was like that. John Dove, a man I'd never heard of, was directing it. I found out afterwards that John had said, 'No way will I work with Eileen Atkins, she would terrify me'. After the first day's rehearsal, John said 'Look, I just want to tell you something. You can say anything to me because I'm not frightened of you.' I didn't know I frightened anybody.

After that we had the most fabulous actor/director relationship because neither of us felt we had to cover anything up or to hand a sweetie to the other person to make them do it. Too many actors are real wilting flowers in rehearsal. I've seen people wilt just because a director has said, 'That's no good'. Well, sometimes it *is* no good, you've got to start again.

There's a little litany I say to myself at every single rehearsal, and it gets worse as I get older. I have to think, 'I am not doing this for the other members of the cast. This is a rehearsal process. I am just working for me and the director. We're just trying to get it right. Don't show off to the others'!

In my mid-thirties, I went to America to learn about being more physical as an actor. I'd got totally fed up with what I called the 'tadpole' actors here who are all head and no body. They are *brilliant* in their minds and their body is incidental. Perversely, I also think that one of the good things that makes British actors very good is this funny sort of repression we have. However, I thought I wasn't using my body enough and I went to America because everything in Britain seemed to be about the head, not about the heart or the guts which is where I want things to come from.

It was revelatory. I think there are some *wonderful* American actors and I think we are *incredibly* snobby about them. The group I did *As You Like It* with at Stratford, Connecticut, were an infinitely better company than at Stratford-upon-Avon, but would any of them believe it? Oh no. Because you bow down and kiss the ground when a British actor walks by. I think they're beginning to come to, a bit, now.

I went to Broadway to do *Vivat! Vivat Regina!* by Robert Bolt. I loved doing it in the beginning because it was huge fun to make work, a nice big canvas and a new play so nobody else had done it. That was wonderful because you just don't get that any more. I'll be lucky if I do another ten new plays before I die. Who's going to write them? It's very rarely that a middle-aged woman is the main interest in a play, except a bit on TV. Even *I* don't particularly want to go and see them. Mostly, if you're telling a tale, the woman is the romantic interest, though not in the parts I've played.

There are hardly any even half-decent plays. You've only got to say in an article, 'there aren't any good parts for women' and you get sent the most dreadful stuff. I get terribly worried. I think the kind of theatre that I like doing is totally going out of fashion. To me, good theatre is almost anything. My favourite evening in the theatre is Barry Humphries. He knows how to have an audience in the palm of his hand and relate to it totally. Brilliant. I'm mad, too, about Marguerite Duras, but she can be tedious at times and, if she directs a play herself, it's a nightmare.

I think words and what one does with them are what is important. What's being said is of primary importance. If the script isn't right, to me it's not interesting. There's no doubt that what people are going to see now are things with wonderful scenery. It's stopped being director's theatre and started being designer's theatre.

I enjoyed doing Virginia Woolf more than anything. I vowed I would never, ever, do a one-woman show. I thought they were tedious and boring. Then, whenever I went, I always enjoyed them. I'd got the rights to do the Vita Sackville-West/Virginia love letters. Then Patrick Garland offered me his adaptation of Virginia's *A Room of One's Own*. When I read it, I realized at once that it worked. There's no story in it, but once you start . . . Virginia's voice is pure heaven.

The awful thing is, when I'm working on something – again, I hope I've got better as I got older – I get so passionate about who I'm playing that for a while I see things only from their point of view. I nearly lost a friend through Virginia. Mostly I feel, oh, to hell with you, but in this case I knew it was chauvinist men who thought they were going to be bored and who automatically thought Virginia Woolf was a bore when she's not. Everybody tends to think of her with those stones in her pocket committing suicide when actually she's *huge fun*.

I've always thought it's awfully camp and boring of people to say so, but I have to admit it – I *do* take my character home. My husband now says, 'What's the character like? I hope I'm going to like living with her for a bit.' I turned down Mrs Morel in *Sons and Lovers* a couple of times. Ian McKellen said to me, 'You know why you're turning it down, don't you? It's because it's your mother. You don't want to play her because then you'll find out you *are* like your mother.' And he was absolutely right. That *is* the reason I didn't want to do it.

The first time I really noticed I was doing it was when I was playing *The Killing of Sister George*. I was absolutely stunned when people came into the dressing room and said, 'Very good, but what a nasty girl she was'. I thought, 'Nasty? You don't understand.' I thought the play was quite funny when I read it. I was desperately out of work at the time, Julian and I were just about to separate and I thought, 'Oh well, it'll fill in at Bristol'. I never thought it would come into the West End. I remember Janet Suzman, Michael Williams and Charlie Kay came to see it in Oxford and afterwards they said, 'You're OK in it but it's not going to work, it's going to be a disaster'. I didn't have any particular feelings about it myself. We all thought the world had opened up and everything was possible. As soon as I got into the theatre, I thought, 'Aha, everybody does everything here'. So it never entered my head there'd be any fuss about it. I thought it was only my parents in Tottenham who had all these ridiculous taboos. I didn't realize the world had them, too.

When it turned out to be such a success, it was very exciting – as it was to work with Beryl Reid who came from a completely different corner of the room. Val May was brilliant; he directed us all totally differently. In rehearsal he would never talk to Beryl about emotion or what she was feeling. He would tell her to lean back on a chair, or sit at a different degree or hold her hands together and, somehow, that was good direction for Beryl. If he'd said that to me, I would have been in despair. I was used to people talking about emotion and motive. Whenever we had any talk like that, Beryl would say, 'Ah well, you two are having one of your chats now, so I'll go and make some phone-calls'.

That's the thing you have to swallow in the theatre – that what's right for you isn't necessarily right for somebody else. People have all kinds of different methods. I think that's the genius of a good director, bringing his orchestra together – 'Oh I see, *he's* very slow and doesn't do anything; *he* does too much' – and somehow all arriving at the starting post at the same time. Who would have thought, for instance, that the chemistry would work with two such totally different people as Beryl and I. Oddly enough, I did *Sister George* in New York when Beryl was ill, with a very good American actress who was far more obviously the part, as I saw it when I read it – a big, heavy woman with great power. She was excellent but the play didn't work at all.

I suppose that's what's nice about acting. It's a bit of a mystery. And it's always a gamble. My father was a gambling man. And I'm a gambler. I can't *bear* to know actually what I'm doing more than a few months ahead. I don't worry about money. I think mean actors, anyway, aren't very good ones. Somehow, you have got to throw it all out on the water and then maybe it'll come back. That's the way it works for me.

I hope people are beginning to understand that actors – serious actors – get paid very little. I was in some Barbara Cartland thing over Christmas, with six lines – it was a week when there'd been some income tax trouble, not remotely my fault, and I had to pay a huge amount. I suddenly had to do almost anything. Even in that situation, I try to be careful. I try to think, it's six lines in some silly melodrama, that's not going to hurt anyone. I have no feelings at all about taking my clothes off. I played Mary Barnes in America, stark naked covered in shit. I think it is absurd of actors to worry about taking their clothes off when they should be totally revealing their soul every night anyway, revealing what is in them.

Acting can get desperately boring. Eight times a week I do not want to do any more. That's why most of us, if we can bear it, will want to work at the National Theatre or the RSC. But the money is appalling.

Sometimes wonderful things *do* happen in theatres and you really feel a tremendous rapport with the audience. Heart-warming is too sentimental a word, it's a celebration of being human and you feel that coming back. Of course, audiences change. I think of it as a big animal out there and each night, it's different. I don't think I woo audiences enough. I go out and say, 'this is what I do', and I try not to alter it for the sake of what I feel coming back to me. But I *do* alter it. I just put in a little bit more to say, 'please, come on, listen to this'. I miss that in television. I always enjoy being among other actors, but it's a different thing just doing it for the camera.

To keep acting a part every night, you have to be con-trolled, but you've had to go through it in an uncontrolled way to achieve that control. That's what's exciting about rehearsals – occasionally you have to go through the actual thing or as near as dammit. And then you have to technically say, 'I see, I did that, that and that', and try and get it back again. Usually you get it fabulously one day in rehearsal and you think, 'My god, I've hit it, I've hit it'.

There's a wonderful story about Larry Olivier when he was playing Othello. Evidently, one night, he was brilliant, took everyone's breath away. He went into another dimension to such an extent that when the curtain came down, the actors spontaneously all lined up to applaud him to his dressing room. He walked through them, looking furious, and slam-med the door in their faces. Derek Jacobi went in and said, 'Now look, don't you behave like that. Do you realize why we're doing it? We're doing it because you were *wonderful* tonight.' And Olivier said, 'I *know*, and I don't know *why*.'

That is the awful thing. You do it one day in rehearsal and

the next day you start and you think, 'I haven't got it, I don't know where it is'. The endless thing you're trying to do as an actor is to forget yourself. In the best performances, you leave yourself behind and you're winging. There is no technique, there is no reason for it. It is just something that happens, sometimes. About three times in my life I've done a performance like that and then I've thought, 'Yes, I was proud of that, that was good tonight'.

PAM ST CLEMENT

'Playing Pat is a bit like wearing an old sock'

credit: pic. Alan Olley

Born Harrow-on-the-Hill. Trained Rose Bruford.

Pam St Clement is best known as Pat Butcher in *EastEnders*. Before that she had many years experience in television series such as the *Onedin Line* and *Angels* (both BBC), LWT's *Enemy at the Door*, *Within These Walls* (prison series), and *Thomas and Sarah*; the original BBC series about the forensic service, *Indelible Evidence*, *Shoestring* and *The Chinese Detective* (all BBC), *Minder*, Yorkshire TV's *Emmerdale Farm* and LWT's *We'll Meet Again*.

She also appeared in several BBC *Play for Today* slots including what she calls 'a gift' – Connie, a middle-aged woman trying to find meaning to her life after her children have grown up in Gilly Frazer's *Not For the Likes of Us*; also William Trevor's three-part Play of the Week, *Matilda's England* (with Anna Calder Marshall).

In theatre, she was a member of Joan Littlewood's company at the Theatre Royal, Stratford East; played Berte in the RSC's World Tour and film of *Hedda Gabler* with Glenda Jackson as Hedda, directed by Trevor Nunn; and Mother Basil in Mary O'Malley's very funny comedy about a Catholic childhood, *Once a Catholic*.

Films include Mai Zetterling's *Scrubbers* and Alan Parker's first feature film, *Our Cissie*.

She lives in London.

The reason I do so much television is very simple. The amount of theatre, in comparison to what is done now in television, has shrivelled horrendously over the last twenty years. This has happened around the world and particularly in Britain under the Tory government. The big theatre companies are having trouble enough, but the little ones are being squeezed out.

When I first went into theatre, there were many Theatre-in-Education (TIE) companies, and they were doing terrific work that really involved kids. I worked with Brian Way's theatre company for some time, taking drama in to schools. Now, kids don't have that sort of exposure at all and, I fear, when this schools' management business comes into full swing, they're likely to have even less experience of drama.

So what's everybody's idea of theatre entertainment now? It's going to a West End show – except for somewhere like Glasgow Citizens' Theatre, whose work, though often seemingly high-brow, draws its audience very much from its locality.

My training ground was the theatre and what stands out for me from those years was the time I spent with Joan Littlewood. She was very good at seeing an actor's blocks. She might not always have known why they were there – although I suspect that very often she did – but she would try and get round them or dig them out. Or frighten them out of you. I think I tended to do what was contradictory to my type and size, to play from the higher part of my body. Joan knew that sometimes we all needed a kick in the guts, in the belly if not the groin. Wonderful woman.

I've had my bad times but some of my friends have had a lot worse. Any actor who said they were always in work would be lying. When I joined Equity there were about 18,000 members. Think how few there must have been when people like Dame Peggy Ashcroft joined. Now the numbers are phenomenal – and there's less work, less proving grounds in the provinces in terms of theatre, less movies. There's more television, of course, because of Channel 4, but in my early days in television there used to be the wonderful classical series and one-off plays. None of that's done any more. One-off plays are too expensive. Everybody wants to make a movie. They can justify the expenditure more, which is a pity because they're not utilizing the studio facilities, though it's true that the studio facility is very cumbersome and unwieldy. Everything tends to be at its mercy. It's a great big machine and eats up time and people as a consequence. It is far better if you can get out with lightweight or hand held cameras, but it costs a lot more money on location.

In the end, as in America, there won't be the studio in Britain. The Americans don't know anything about our studio technique. They look completely baffled when they get taken to the BBC Centre at Elstree. Sitcoms like *Roseanne* are done on sound stages. *Cagney and Lacey* is done with interior sets. They aren't studio, they're the real thing or are specially built, rather as they are on the back-lot of Pinewood Studios. *EastEnders* is all on tape.

My first television job was a very small part in a play for BBC2. Fortunately, I had the common sense to sit back and learn and watch the experienced ones. It wasn't for about four years after that that I was able to look at it with some sort of objectivity and see the technique that was involved. Before that, I'd be acting my socks off – absolutely doing my nut and there was no camera on me! I didn't understand that because I was used to theatre. I started to realize there was a technique to this. You don't have to be camera conscious but there's an element somewhere that tells you when that eye is watching you. You don't have that on film because on film it's just your relationship to one eye which is why it's so gorgeous.

There's a light on the camera but I would hesitate to tell anybody ever to be aware of that. It's something you find you can do when you've had enough experience and I knew that I'd had enough the first time I picked up a camera script and realized that I could cope with it.

* * *

I've always played older than myself because I've always had an ample figure. Young people aren't meant to have ample figures and also large people are meant to be battle-axes as well. Strangely enough, I wasn't stereotyped, perhaps because people saw me and then thought 'no'. I may have the Peggy Mount appearance but I'm really much gentler than that.

Pat in *EastEnders* is certainly no softie. I first came into *EastEnders* in May 1986, eighteen months after it had started. Playing Pat is a bit like wearing an old sock really. I've got used to wearing her now. I didn't come in as a regular, I came in for a couple of episodes to create turmoil – which indeed I did. Having done that and been a real, venomous bitch to my ex-husband's then current wife, I disappeared back to the man I was living with, Mr Wicks. I really was the slag of all slags.

When I was asked back, Julia Smith, the executive producer who created the whole thing, said 'We'd like the character to come back. Let's talk about it, and we'll think about the regularity of it'. I said, 'How could that character possibly fit into a community?'

I did cause havoc at first but I've been very lucky with the character because I've slowly been allowed to develop it. Pat is very streetwise and very protective of her own, very defensive because she is vulnerable. She's vulnerable because she has been used by men, mostly. Or hasn't chosen the men for the right reasons. I have a suspicion that Pat was probably put on the wrong track in her youth and, brought up in the fifties and sixties, probably suffered from peer group pressure.

It says in the script that she was a stunner when she was younger. I think she probably found it very easy to get what she wanted from men by saying 'yes', and got a bad name. It's the old thing with men. You give them what they want and then you're a slag. You can't win. That's the trail Pat probably started on and it just went from worse to worse. I think I could fairly say that my character has travelled thirty years' worth of experience and personal development. Thirty years in three years, but drama is condensed anyway, so I think that's valid. As actors, we all have to tread a very fine line between what we think is morally correct and politically correct and actually remembering that we are portraying other folk, not ourselves. If you want to do the latter, maybe you should be somewhere else. That doesn't mean to say you can't change people's attitudes.

Actors are relatively powerless people in the creative process. We are mouthpieces for writer's words. It's an ongoing argument as to whether art should reflect life – I know people say it's the other way round – or whether it's there to educate. I think there must be a fine balance. I would hesitate, in a soap, to do anything which I thought was not resolved. I think that's why I always liked *EastEnders* before I came into it because I felt that the problems that came up, as far as is possible in life, were resolved, even if it was only facing up to the fact that you can't resolve it.

I always felt that *EastEnders* did that and I liked that about it. They tackled the nitty-gritty but not gratuitously. Things weren't put there – drugs or whatever – just for the sake of it. It tries to portray life, not always in a very pleasant way, because life isn't always very pleasant.

A woman rang up on a chat show I did. She'd been watching the episode when Den's body was fished out of the canal and asked, didn't we think that was rather unpleasant? If a youngster had just switched on, wouldn't that be a bad way to start their viewing with the series and upsetting? Actually, the body was never seen. And, unfortunately, those things do happen. Worse things happen every day in the *Sun* – suggestions, horrific headlines, sensational phrases which get the imagination going much more than somebody saying 'oh, it's him', seeing the funeral and then that's it.

I've only once drawn the line. It was when Den had left me in charge of the pub and disappeared, and I was very harassed. I was trying to hold the pub together, and the dog was bothering me. The script dictated that I open the front door, get hold of the dog's collar, turn him round out of the front door and say, 'Go and play with one of Chris Smith's lorries'.

I went up to the office and said, 'I know that the writer has written this as a bit of a joke line, but you do realize that this is going out in the middle of August and I am certainly not giving our viewers permission to chuck their dogs off on the motorway.' They said, 'You're absolutely right. There are other ways of doing it.' In the end, I used another line – 'Go and play with that rat of a master of yours' – which still kept to the character because I didn't want to make the character sympathetic.

This is the problem. Nowadays you've got thinking actors. You never used to be allowed to think as an actor. Now every actor thinks that they're Einstein, which is terribly dangerous sometimes because they can't always dissect what's the character and what's them. Also lots of actors do want to be loved. Little do they realize that audiences actually love villains. Dirty Den was the biggest shit in the world and everybody loved him.

Something like *EastEnders* burns you out at a fast rate. There are other things I want to do, other parts and perhaps other aspects of work. It will be very interesting to see what happens when I come out of the series. It's never easy coming out of a long-running series like this. In Britain, we hate success – if someone's been successful, knock 'em down.

In America, if you've been in a soap for a while, a producer will come along and say, 'Great, let's have her in this because that will put bums on seats'. The audience will immediately know that person and say, 'I'll go and watch that film because so and so is in it'. For the first three minutes, they'll be saying, 'He's Bobby in *Dallas*', but after the three minutes, they'll quite happily fall into the character you're playing. In Britain, it seems to me that the powers that be that cast film, theatre or television won't give you the chance to explore. They always underestimate the audience.

I want to keep on working but also doing things that interest me. It still gives me pleasure or I wouldn't do it, it's too much like heartache. I think the pleasure is probably losing yourself, exploring those things that are within yourself, through somebody else. I like to explore everything. I've played a nun, I've virtually played a tart, and everything between the two. I'm a gay woman but I play a married woman in *EastEnders*, just as I'd play Lizzie Borden or, if I was a man, Othello, even if I hadn't murdered anyone. I play a married woman because married people are part of the fabric of our society. In fact, I was married for seven years.

When I became a regular member of *EastEnders*, I had to make a judgement about how to 'play it' – being gay – even though there were several people in the company and also on the production side of this particular show who know me and know my circumstances. I was perfectly open about it because if you can't be open in this business, what business can you be open in?

I'd seen what the press did to several members of *EastEnders* when it first started. It's a very high-profile show and, knowing the way such tabloids as the *Sun* have started to move in the last few years, their methods and what they're after, I had to make a decision. I spoke to the people closest to me, and said, 'I really think the best thing to do is for me not to say anything. I'm not going to pretend to be what I'm not because I'm surrounded by people who know my background. But likewise, I'm not going to make a song and dance about it'.

That was fine – for a year, eighteen months.

Then I got a telephone call from friends in Norfolk – I had a place there then – saying, 'The press are here, sniffing around, asking questions about you'. Warning bells went. I had been planning to go up there that weekend but decided not to. They caught up with me just the same. They were on the doorstep, shouting through the letter box, 'We're going to publish anyway, we want to talk to you about this that and the rest of it'. It became front page *News of the World*.

They were wonderful on *EastEnders*. My screen husband, an old-fashioned macho man, was really lovely. He sent flowers to me and my partner. I was also contacted by my ex-husband who was most sympathetic and concerned on my behalf. For a while, I did have people being rather troublesome round my house, youths standing outside shouting things. But it was a nine-day wonder, really. The only thing was, 'it' was seen by a lot more people than it would normally have been because it was on the front page.

Once I sat back and thought about it and got over the sheer anger at their inaccuracy and bias – they tried to make my lover into a Radclyffe Hall character; it said, 'lives with big butch lover' and she's like eight stone and a willow – I decided to keep a dignified silence. Lots of people said to me, 'You did the right thing. It really is not worth being provoked by people like that.' If you respond to it, they're provoking you into doing something which simply then earns them more pennies. You're just promoting their circulation.

I think the BBC play a sort of waiting game with me. They

knew where they stood with Michael Cashman because he was so totally and completely politically committed. With me, they got a bit edgy when I did *The Media Show* and when I was asked to do *Out on Tuesday*. You have to realize with the Beeb, it's not just that I was doing something political. I was doing it for the other side – ITV – as well! You can't imagine anybody from *Coronation Street* doing a promotion on the BBC. *EastEnders* is very much an ambassador for the BBC, the current flagship in terms of drama serials. So we do have to be very careful.

The reason the whole thing happened was because of Clause 28. There was a benefit at the Piccadilly Theatre – one of the most wonderful evenings of my life. Michael Cashman said, 'Ian McKellen and I would love you to do something, to be involved in it. It's up to you whether you do.' We'd already decided that a certain number of us were interested in doing something as a group, so we did the *EastEnders* sketch. But Michael said to me, 'It won't stop there. You do realize what you're taking on board.' And I said, 'There's a certain point beyond which I won't go. I'm making a stand and I don't care what happens.' After the thing at the Piccadilly, I was walking back to my car in Soho and this young man came running up and said, 'Miss St Clement? Press. I just want to ask you why you're involved in this Clause 28.' I said, 'Look, I'm in a hurry, I'm going to my car because I'm going on somewhere else.' I gave him a one-liner about freedoms and actors and making a stand and that was it. But I swear that's where it started, that's where they got their first sniff.

I took the stance in full knowledge. I don't mind, I can cope with it. I don't talk about it any more than the others talk about what they do at home with whoever they live with. The thing is, I wasn't in the closet. Because I was in a high-profile programme, I felt that, for the sake of those nearest and dearest and for the programme, I wouldn't make a song and dance about it. I wouldn't have done any more had I been three times divorced because it wouldn't have been necessary and it deflects from what you're doing.

Likewise, I have always been hesitant to be labelled ever since. I don't want to go on a programme that just wants to talk about my sexuality. Like everything else in an actor's life, there should be a lot that is left shrouded in mystery. Once you've peeled away the layers and shown the mechanics, you have no mystery – and theatre, my business, is all about that. I don't want people to know the bare bones of things. That immediately takes away from where you can go. You're made finite because you're compartmentalized.

I am 'out' and the fact that I am in the position I'm in gives a lot of encouragement to people that I go and see – Gaysocs and things like that. But I'm certainly not going to metaphorically wave a banner over Elstree and say everybody's got to be gay. I think we ought to stop worrying so much.

Michael Cashman and Ian McKellen have been very understanding and very compassionate in that they have actually faced the fact that, even in an environment like show business where one isn't a pariah, they still recognize that, with a gay woman, there's a sort of underlying joke – even if it isn't quite as base as 'she can't get a man'. The men have their own little club somehow.

I still think 'outing' is a very doubtful method altogether. It wouldn't have made any difference to me because I was actually at one with myself in terms of where I was at. It didn't make any difference that a stinking tabloid had to do it. I was there already.

There aren't that many portrayals of lesbians on screen, or anywhere else, but I prefer that rather than their being portrayed badly. *The Killing of Sister George*, for example, was a very funny, beautifully written play which didn't do anything for the cause. I would hate to see it revived. We've gone through that, we've got to go further.

What is this complete hang-up about sex anyway? We're *obsessed* with it in this country. Maybe men are the ones who are hung up on it – they've got to prove themselves and all that – and, as a consequence, women get hung up. I find I relate to people personally rather than whatever their biology is; I actually do get on very well with men. When I'm working with directors, I might like working with a woman director because of the notes she gives, and I might like the man because of his ideas. But whatever it is, I have the confidence and I'm happy enough with myself to say things if I need to.

The response amongst people here at *EastEnders* to Jeanette Winterson's *Oranges are not the only Fruit* was amazing. People watched that and cared about the folk in it. They cared about the people, what they wanted out of life, where their hearts were, not about their sexuality or where their sex organs were. The things that work so beautifully are tackling the epic qualities of life – jealousy, love – which is why Shakespeare has lasted.

Maybe *EastEnders* is not Shakespeare but Shakespeare was writing for an audience we now work to! Perhaps there's too much preciousness in theatre now. Nothing can beat live theatre, getting up on a stage, but I don't treat the theatre as the great god – as many people do – simply because I'm very sorry that theatre in Britain is in the parlous state it is at the moment, particularly for women. Janet Suzman is a good example. I don't know how she has the patience with the theatre in Britain. The level of work she has achieved and what she does should mean that work comes flooding to her door.

In theatre, you've got that heritage of work which has been very male biased. Shakespeare has a lot to answer for, on that score! An actress friend of mine once had a Shakespeare party, and the condition of the party was that the women came as male, and the men came as female characters. One of her actor friends rang and said, 'I'm having such trouble. I mean there's only a handful of women I can choose from.' She replied: 'It's a party for you, dear – for us, it's our lives.'

JANET SUZMAN

'Not so much a profession as an obsession'

Born South Africa. Graduate of Witwatersrand University, trained LAMDA in London.

Janet Suzman has long been regarded as one of Britain's finest classical actresses whose performances of such roles as Cleopatra, Hedda Gabler and Masha (for which she won the *Evening Standard* Best Actress award in 1976) have now come to be regarded by many as definitive.

A member of the RSC from 1962–73 – 'it was my cradle', she once said in an interview, 'I was weaned there' – she first came to public attention as a fiery Joan of Arc in the 1960s Peter Hall/John Barton's history trilogy, *The Wars of the Roses*. During her years with them, she played most of Shakespeare's leading female roles and subsequently such other classics as the Duchess of Malfi, Brecht's Shen Te in *The Good Person of Sichuan* and Racine's Andromache. She also played Clytemnaestra and Helen of Troy in the RSC's *The Greeks* season in 1980.

Since then, she has starred in the plays of fellow South Africans, Athol Fugard's *Hello and Goodbye* with Ben Kingsley, *Boesman and Lena* with Stuart Wilson, and last year, Ronald Harwood's *Another Time* with Albert Finney, Sara Kestelman and David de Keyser.

Film credits include *A Day in the Death of Joe Egg* with Alan Bates, Peter Greenaway's *The Draughtsman's Contract*, *A Dry White Season* with Donald Sutherland and Marlon Brando, *Nicholas and Alexandra* and Fellini's *E La Nave Va*. Television appearances have included Hedda, Arnold Bennett's *Clayhanger* and Dennis Potter's *The Singing Detective*.

In 1988, she returned to South Africa to direct *Othello* at the Market Theatre in Johannesburg (televised in Britain the following Christmas), and in 1990 directed Michael Hastings's *A Dream of People* for the RSC. Her aunt is the veteran civil-rights campaigner, Helen Suzman, who elsewhere has described Janet Suzman as 'a very political animal'.

She was married to the director, Trevor Nunn, for seventeen years and now lives in London with their small son, Joshua.

I always trailed around after my elder brother. I was two years younger than him and made his life a misery, as far as I've been told. I played with his friends and they tolerated me the way older boys do. I was quite a toughie. I climbed trees and wanted to bat at cricket but was never allowed to. Being brought up in South Africa, we were always outdoors and, when I became adolescent and began to perceive the world from other dimensions, my inspiration was always to do with the landscapes of Africa and I have remained affected by them.

I certainly had no acting ambitions of any kind at that time, although there were a lot of American musicals that arrived on tour. One was *Oklahoma*. Another was *Annie Get Your Gun*, which took us all by storm. I saw them both about six or seven times. I'd never seen such wonderful stuff! I remember once seeing a touring production of *A Midsummer Night's Dream*, with Irene Worth as Titania and Paul Rogers as Bottom. And I remember Margot Fonteyn doing *Swan Lake* with Johannesburg City Ballet, and Bengiamino Gigli coming to give recitals. Otherwise, it was a cultural desert. There were, of course, the summer festivals. My aunt ran a theatre in Cape Town, a beautiful outdoor theatre called Maynardville, and every summer we had to go and see her productions of Shakespeare in the open air.

I started acting by accident when I was at university. I joined the drama society because, as in most universities, it seemed to have the best time. Round about the end of my second year, which was much more taken up with things political, I did get the feeling that I'd like to know more about acting, but my parents said, quite properly, 'You finish your degree my girl', which I did. Then I flew to England on an arts faculty tour which was the cheapest fare I could find. I landed up in London. Somebody told me that you had to get a copy of Spotlight's *Contacts* and write to every drama school that advertises. I knew nothing and when you know nothing you are wonderfully arrogant. My parents were very sceptical, but when I'd actually been accepted – much to my surprise – by RADA, Central School and LAMDA, they said, 'OK, you might as well do it'.

I must say, after my first *day* at LAMDA, I felt a great weight had lifted from my shoulders – that *agony*, when you're young, of not knowing what to do with yourself, of not really knowing what you want to become. The fact that I had auditioned and had got in made me feel that I was doing the right thing.

I'm not exactly what you would call a middle-class actress because I'm a foreigner, which gives me more freedom. I'm pretty rootless, which probably goes with the idea that actors should be gypsies. They're not, in fact.

The acting profession is as many branched as, say, medicine. In that sense, I suppose I'm a specialist. I have elected to concentrate more on a specific area of the drama which is called classical. I am more interested – or have been up to now – in classical plays. They make my blood run quicker. Now the classical parts are more expandable; there's no right way of doing them, no definitive way. Whoever does them has their own thing to contribute. A bad play, I think, is more one-dimensional and you don't have so much room for movement. There's inherent elasticity in a good play.

I have a very low boredom quotient and I knew, when I left drama school, that if I was going to be addressing texts that were basically uninteresting, I would lose interest. I'm a terrible snob about writing. From my first day at drama school, I didn't see any point in being an actress unless I could bump my shins up against the great texts. One of the few places you can come across the great texts is Stratford. It's terribly boring up there but that's where you get the texts. Still, at this great age, when people ask what other plays I want to do, I think, well now, there's O'Casey and I haven't done O'Neill . . . I'm still instinctively looking towards major texts. Not that it stopped me doing films like *Nicholas and Alexandra*. Fame, money, Hollywood – God, a big movie! How could I resist that? Snobbism, in my book, doesn't extend to that kind of pursed-lips attitude.

Sometimes you have a secret little yen for something in your career. Arnold Bennett's Hilda Lessways in *Clayhanger* is mine – a hidden-away favourite. It was one of the first times that a novel had been put on to television, word for word, page by page, something horrific like twenty-four episodes. Faithfulness to the original was total. I played this sparky little character who made everybody's life a total misery – maybe a very minor Hedda character because she, too, was kicking against the traces of conformity and domesticity. I think ITV considered it a bit of a bore, but it developed a kind of cult following. I thought it was very brave of them, it's the kind of thing English television occasionally comes up with, literary and interesting. They've never done it again.

Is it pure accident that I haven't done much popular stuff? I think everybody is a saleable object and, if you're going to fulfil a generic role – pubkeeper, housewife, district nurse – or whatever archetypal characters you're bound to have to step in to in a soap opera, then physically or in terms of background, in some way that's what you need to be to be completely believable. I'm not that saleable, I guess, not being an English type. Is it pure accident, for example, that Penelope Keith found herself veering towards those upper middle-class creatures simply because she assumed that persona, looked it, dressed it and sounded it, and therefore she's believable in it? She also has that extra, instinctive edge of comedy that makes her such a wonderful exponent of those sorts of parts. But to begin with the shape was right, the sound was right.

So, I don't think casting is just 'looks' – it's what you seem to carry with you. Good casting is 70 per cent of any production in television or theatre. It's probably 90 per cent of film casting. Get the casting right and you're well on the way to getting everything right.

Some actors like to be a moving target. I'm in that area. I don't want to be typed. People do like definition, but this actor prefers to defy definition because that keeps the options more open.

There are quite a few Shakespeare parts I wish I had played when I was younger. If I were now twenty-two, I'd like to play Juliet, Imogen and *All's Well*. But would *I* have cast me as Juliet? I don't think I look much like a Juliet. These are preconceptions which people have. I don't know where they come from, out of some received collective unconscious about what certain characters should look like, I suppose. We're told Falstaff is fat, so he has to be fat. We're not told much about other dramatic characters, but people seem to have an idea, all the same.

When I directed *Othello* in South Africa, I cast John Kani as Othello. John is a small man. I had to fight *every* preconception. The Othelloid idea has been of a vast, chesty individual. I think it's rather stock playing. The case for small generals is watertight, from Alexander the Great onwards. I read so many notices saying what a pity he was so small. It wasn't a pity at all. I wanted a guerrilla fighter, a tough, small, compact man.

Actors are eternally optimistic. It's the thing that probably differentiates us from other brands of human being. Every time you embark on a project you truly believe that you can contribute towards it and that, just maybe, it'll be OK. When I was fresh out of drama school, I went to Sheffield where there were some very old actors hanging on by their teeth. It so frightened me, the thought of being ancient and in Sheffield and still playing small parts in rep, that I made a vow to myself then and there that if I hadn't achieved something that I considered OK by the time I was thirty, I would change profession.

Acting requires, for its very life, a kind of selfishness. You have to defend your character's patch. People see the world through their own eyes, *their* version of *their* story – that's the version that you have to examine when you're doing a play.

I'd forgotten how brave acting is. Since directing, my estimation of actors has gone up. Actors don't think they're brave but they are. From the other side of the fence, as a director, you see the kind of things you're asking them to do – and then they do it. Wow! Chancing their arm, sticking their neck out . . .

The safety you feel doing extraordinarily intimate things on stage – like bearing your soul – is because it's the character's dilemma. It's the old conundrum of truth-telling. You tell the truth when you have a disguise upon you, that's what all the fools do in Shakespeare. Truth-telling can only properly be done when you are well disguised. That is the only reason to be an artist: to try to tell the truth. That is what a complex text is about – appearance and reality. It's the same in front of a camera. The great screen actors view that camera as an intimate. Stage actors view the audience as an intimate.

You hear that some directors don't think all that much of actors, that they are there only to serve their ends. That's often said of movies. Hitchcock simply wanted the creature he wanted; he had no time to discuss acting. That's probably the way movies are best served. Theatre and film are not comparable. The thing you have to do for a camera is behave, just 'be'.

We should never underestimate the influence of the movies in this century. Close-ups have affected both actors and audience in the theatre, which is one reason why small-house productions have become so popular. People want to see the whites of the eyes. Those enormous proscenium theatres built by the Victorians and Edwardians in Glasgow, Leeds, Birmingham and so on, do make acting rather different. The *luxury* of intimacy in smaller theatres! It's much easier, I've no doubt, to make great reckonings in little rooms. The sheer wattage given off by a crowd of talented people in a small space is pretty overwhelming. That is much more elusive in a very large space. I'm sure I would find some primal excitement in the acting of Edmund Kean and Sarah Bernhardt because of the electricity they generated, but I would also probably find them ludicrous. La Duse is the only one who would now come out OK for our tastes because she was very simple, real and economical.

On the whole, the feeling of rightness has stayed with me. There are, of course, moments when I think, 'Why am I doing this piece, get me out of this'. It is, by no means, unalloyed pleasure. You spend much more of your time dissatisfied with yourself than the other way round. And sometimes the *struggle* to get something right is dreadful; there is an absolutely definable feeling of self-*distrust*. You know perfectly well when you haven't got hold of it, and when you *have* got hold of it, you also know. That is the feeling one is always striving for because, once you've got something right, you can't do it wrong. You could stand on your head and it would still be right. Of course, you may do a performance which isn't quite so vivid, when the juices just aren't there. It's very difficult to do it every time, eight times a week. It's an insane way of asking human animals to perform. You have to find a way of doing the same thing night after night or you go off your rocker.

A long run is something rather new to me. There's a wonderful point in a play when you know it thoroughly – backwards, inside out, upside down. Then your freedom to invent increases. There are all sorts of nice inspirations once you've got hold of the character. You'll find yourself doing a speech a different way. If you have rapport with somebody, things change all the time. It's very exhilarating, like playing a good game of tennis.

Sometimes there can be a terrific zing on stage and absolutely nothing between you at all off stage. Or vice versa. The theatre's famous for that. When you take your fantasy out of the stage door, that's bedlam time.

The point about art is that you address it at the time you should, which is in your work area. One of the disciplines you learn as a young actor, for example, is not to bring your personal troubles into the rehearsal room. It's nobody's business except yours. What you're there to do is address the work in hand. By all means, use your personal troubles as an artist, but keep it private. It's your own particular, internal pathway. Actors get better as they get older because they've got more life under their belt. Your imagination is freer as you get older. You've lived more and, after all, that's your tool.

The Chekhovs and Ibsens are thrilling to play, bottomless, like the Bay of Portugal. There are two favourite parts that I've been able to approach at separate moments in my life. One is Masha in *Three Sisters*, and the other one is Hedda Gabler. I've played them both twice. It's not often that you can play one of the great parts twice these days.

I first did Hedda on television for the BBC and, some

years later, I did it on stage. That was very interesting because they were both quite different. The first Hedda was cheekier, more amused, more insolent. The second was much more a victim of her own passions, more helpless. Events moved her more than she moved events. All that energy and efficiency, and nowhere to put it – the tragedy of domesticity. Hedda's would naturally be a creative mind were it put on the right paths.

The moment you have family obligations, you take upon you the mantle of *all* womanhood. The only way you can free yourself of that is to be like a man and not have a child. With a child, you become completely taken over. That's why the debate about whether Hedda is pregnant or not is stupid. Of course she is. That's what she feels, that's what she knows. It's a male debate: 'Is she or isn't she?' She understands exactly what it implies – loss of freedom.

Actresses with children spend their time in a continual state of *desperate* guilt about leaving their children too much. The days of Gypsy Rose Lee toting her children around in laundry boxes and putting them in the wings has gone. Now we feel they've got to be properly at school every day and not whizzed hither and yon into some theatre or another. We've become over-conformist and respectable. We're like any working women except acting is not so much a profession as an obsession. You can't *half* rehearse.

Most other sorts of jobs, you can be back in the evening for the children. You don't need to have that *spotlit* inner concentration that you do when you're creating a role. The only time I've ever experienced complete clarity of mind was when I was directing *Othello* in Johannesburg and, consequently, my little boy was staying with my mother, who took on my role. I knew it was going to be fine and therefore my mind cleared. It was absolutely wonderful. I understood for the *first* time what men must feel when they close the door on their loving wife and know everything's going to be looked after. Women can't usually do that. They're *always* rushing out during the lunch hour to do the shopping, worried that the kid is this, that or the next thing. You crave that release. The mind needs to be disburdened to be *really* creative. I remember seeing an article by Elizabeth Lutyens, the composer, saying something like, 'My children took up all my time. I had lots of symphonies inside me that I couldn't get out'. That I understand *completely*.

Still, having a child is the best thing I've ever done. It's for real, your feet are in the clay. You're part of the great bloody stream of life. Anything that expands your feelings and sensibilities, as having a child does, feeds into your work. Maybe nobody else on earth notices it but I do – I'm definitely better at my job, post-child than pre-child. I've much more feeling to draw on because having a child turns you inside out and also your sense of priorities is *blissfully* simplified – there is nothing more important than your child. It's a great relief to put yourself low down on the list. When you start rehearsing a play, the character becomes your child and you defend it as tigerishly.

At a recent rehearsal, we had a male director and a male writer – two males in unassailable positions, quite often the norm. I was playing the mother. At a certain point in rehearsal, I was asking whys and wherefores about her character and the author said, 'She just is awful. She just argues. That's what she does'. And I said, 'Now just hang on a minute. I'm going to stand up for this mother. There must be a reason for the arguments, which possibly you haven't bothered with, but I shall find out.'

Now, is that just a working situation? Or is it a woman saying, 'You men, you just generalize about women'? It's blurred at that point. I think it's probably more a slight tinge of Janet getting a bit cross with the men, maybe that's 25 per cent of it. But 75 per cent of it will be Janet the actress saying, 'Just go away, I've got some work to do'. The point is you mustn't stand in judgement on your character, although you don't necessarily have to empathize.

I've played two parts that have been anathema to me, politically speaking: the Empress Alexandra of Russia in the film *Nicholas and Alexandra*, and an Afrikaner wife in *A Dry White Season*. Both these two women are as far away from me as is possible, but you use your imagination to find the things that affect *all* humanity – which in these two cases was a child. The way in that I found both times, once before I had a child of my own and once after, was the same way. I understood Alexandra's obsession with her little son's haemophilia. It was on that foundation *only* that I built a blinkered woman, who couldn't see anything outside the nursery. As for the Afrikaner woman, she couldn't bear to compromise her child's future. There are always human bits lurking in people you can't understand, though in daily life, putting yourself in somebody else's shoes seems to be the most difficult thing in the world for people to do.

For a woman, things become more problematic after the age of forty. It's not just the getting of roles – it's the writing. There just aren't any roles. Where are the King Lears and Coriolanuses for *us*? What do *we* do? If you are good at something, it's a very nice feeling to explore that facility. In fact, as you get older, your imaginative juices get better, more elastic. You've learned more, you're able to deploy your weaponry rather better, you learn conservation, economy.

Acting is not to do with success. It's about something quite the opposite – inner standards. If you're good and fame goes with it, that's a bonus, but I don't view fame as an end in itself. There's a great deal more self-questioning as you go on, not less. Successful performers can afford to choose more carefully what they play. What's sad is that there's not much choice in the big stuff and that's frustrating.

Practically all roles are subordinate to men, even in Shakespeare, which is why I find Act V, scene ii of *Antony and Cleopatra* so appealing. This is the one place in which Cleopatra comes into her own after Antony has died. But still her behaviour is determined by another man – Caesar. Her only way out is to kill herself. With Fugard's plays *Boesman and Lena* and *Hello and Goodbye*, you feel a great respect for women coming out of them. Fugard loves women and understands this Camus-like life-force that enables women to go on. He's a great classical writer in the sense that the only real definition of a classic is that it goes on speaking freshly and doesn't die the death once it's done. Classics don't have to be old; they're modern as well and certainly Fugard is one of the greatest. For twenty-five years, he's been in the forefront, amongst that very select group of major modern writers – Pinter, Beckett, Albee.

In a sense, you're just as good as the last thing you did. That should be the case. But very often a body of work builds up behind you and then indifferent work is viewed as good. One of the hardest things is living up to those standards going on inside you.

There's an important ingredient in acting, which is not minding being disliked as the character you're playing. There's a nice story about Edith Evans who refused to play Lady Macbeth because she couldn't understand, she said, the lady's 'lack of hospitality'. The desire to be loved by the audience is a very dangerous hazard which we can all fall into. We can get rather too nice, too sentimental as a performer. An uncompromising performance is, occasionally, very exhilarating.

I think I am probably considered troublesome, a pain in the arse in rehearsals. If you have questions to ask, you must ask them. When I was directing, I *urged* my cast: if ever there was a point at which they didn't understand what they were doing and wanted to ask a question, they must. It was *their* responsibility.

I had the luck, when I started out, to be in a sort of democratic organization. It was much more like a sort of university common room, a seminar, going on in Stratford. But I had been to university and I was used to open debate and questioning. That was encouraged, especially by John Barton. So interfering, speaking up, was part of my daily way of functioning. I couldn't understand keeping quiet and I still don't understand it – more fool me! When we did *Three Sisters* with Jonathan Miller, which we did in three weeks, it was a free-for-all and extremely fruitful. Everybody spoke up, everybody gave ideas. There again, Miller's an academic, he's used to discussion.

If you become an actor, you are *inevitably* going to deal with difficult texts and I think you must have some foundation from which to approach them. It's quite peculiar how obedient actors are – stifling their natural curiosity and doing what the director tells them to do. But then, there are some directors who actually believe they have this god-like function.

The only time that I've obeyed slavishly was when I worked with Fellini for a week in Rome. I was so aware that he knew infinitely better than me what he was wanting to achieve, I did exactly what he wanted me to do. But that was Fellini – a genius.

Essentially, I'm just a jobbing actor, a jobbing director. I'm not an *auteur*. I work with the material I'm given and, as I'm a writer worshipper, everything springs from the text. The better it is, the more fun you have. I have made some stupid mistakes but that's all right, you've got to make some. I usually struggle with scripts, put them down and walk about and have a cigarette. It's all a bit hazardous.

It was an excellent experience for me, stuck in Britain for so many years, to go and do *Othello* in South Africa. The difference was remarkable. Out of a cast of twenty, I had only four experienced actors. It put a lot of things back into perspective in my own mind. They were avid for help, for me to help them, for them to help each other, for everybody to help everybody else. There was no money at all and we did a very big production in a terribly short space of time. It was very important as a lesson in back to basics, in how much people struggle in most other corners, except for those blessed plots of the big subsidized companies where there's money and experience.

Poor theatre – and I mean poor – brings home to you how blessed we are with an enlightened arts funding policy here. Wrong. It *was* enlightened, it's now much darkened after these years of Thatcher ignorance. If one is forced to think in these demeaning City terms, then it's as well to recall that the theatre industry is one of the rare ones that delivers its product on time.

What makes me cross is the prevailing idea that art (with a small 'a') should be considered cost effective as if it produced light bulbs programmed to give in after so many hours of shedding light in the gloom of our spiritual lives. The Market Theatre in Johannesburg was forced by politics to accept only private donations. State subsidy was tainted by the regime which engendered it, and accepting it would thereby have lost the trust of the black artists whose place of work it was and is. But my! How it struggles to keep its head above water. On the dress rehearsal of *Othello*, I was pleading for a handkerchief. When we made the television version of it, we could afford only five days to film it in. The usual span would be three weeks for a three-hour play. The most important shift of thinking, and the most irreparably damaging, is that if the performing arts become answerable to corporation man they will take on the banality of corporation man.

Look at American television or the lack of coherent theatre product in that country. What an irony it is that visiting business bigwigs are taken to the Royal Opera House to sweat through what is now quite beyond the pockets of those whose passion the opera is. The only American model the government should emulate is that of tax breaks for sponsored arts funding. As for cutbacks in education – I can't begin to express my dismay. If we don't have literacy, we don't have theatre. It's a language medium.

One of the difficulties, after the Market Theatre experience, is to find how to make theatre important here, for me. Everything seemed important there. Directing was very liberating because I have that sort of analytical mind. I never felt, when I started directing, that I was doing anything out of the ordinary. I didn't actually feel I was breaking a mould or crossing a Rubicon. It just seemed like a natural extension of what I've probably been doing in my head for years. It seems to me to be quite a common thing for actors to do now. Head and shoulders above most of them is Joan Littlewood whom we don't see any more – an iconoclast, an original spirit. There are fewer women directors because there are fewer women anything, I suppose.

I think the big trouble for women is if we have an intelligence and a bit of a brain. There is a very peculiar streak of anti-intellectualism in Britain which is also wrong because, if you have the brain, you're not necessarily intellectual, you might just simply be intelligent or articulate. But these become minuses rather than pluses. Women spend a lot of time hiding the fact that they understand something because they don't want to be thought brainy. I remember a friend of mine, a rather glamorous actress who stopped acting years ago, saying, 'It's a terrible thing, to have the mind of a man in the body of a woman'.

This is why reactions, for instance, to someone like Glenda Jackson are edgy. It makes me crazy the way people talk about 'strong women'. You actually ask yourself, 'What is a strong woman?' Bette Davis, Joan Crawford – they're just intelligent women who wished *not to be used*. That is a form of integrity.

I've been asked so often, what are these strong parts you play? I say, 'Just a minute, what you're looking at are the great parts in English dramatic literature.' Obviously they are great pieces of dramatic literature precisely because they are continuously renewable and reinterpretable. So how can they just be this one thing, 'strong'? They're much more complex than that, just as human beings are much more complex. 'Strong' makes you think of biceps. That's not what these characters are about. Both Hedda and Cleopatra kill themselves. Is that strength?

The greatest insult in life is to be misjudged. As an artist, the greatest insult to your characters is for *them* to be misjudged, which is one of the reasons why one is chary of critics. That's why you stop reading reviews. You have to go your own way.

I've played a great many parts that I wanted to. If I was on my deathbed and somebody said, 'What do you wish you had played?', if I still wished I'd played Hedda and Cleopatra and Masha and Hester and Lena, I'd die the poorer. Certainly, it's a much more interesting exercise to play something that is much too big for you. All of them have stretched me. I have been very privileged to play some of the great parts and they really are what makes it all worthwhile.

MEERA SYAL

'I feel I've got a niche here'

Born Wolverhampton.

Meera Syal first came to the fore while still at university with *One of Us*, her one-woman show (co-written with Jacqui Shapiro) which looked at racism through the eyes of a Brummy Asian girl.

Regular performer on the fringe with appearances in plays by Sue Townsend, Elizabeth Bond, Debbie Horsfield, Sarah Daniels, Phil Young, Farroukh Dhondy and Harwaint Bains. Played Jacintha Condor in Caryl Churchill's lethal comedy about the City, *Serious Money* at the Royal Court, in the West End and New York. Other highlights: Rani in Stephen Frears' *Sammy and Rosie Get Laid* (screenplay by Hanif Kureishi), Mrs Candour in *School for Scandal* at Bristol Old Vic, *My Girl* by Barrie Keeffe at Stratford East, Declan Donnellan's production of *Peer Gynt* at the National.

On television, she has appeared in such series as *The Bill* and *Black Silk*; also LWT's *To Have and To Hold* by Deborah Moggach, and most recently, *Kinseys* with Leigh Lawson.

She has contributed as a writer to *Black Silk* (BBC), Radio 4's *Citizens* and *Tandoori Nights* (Channel 4). Her eleven-minute film *A Nice Arrangement* was shown on Channel 4 and her new screenplay, *Sister/Wife*, for the BBC, is to be screened later this year.

She is married to journalist Shekhar Bhatia and they live in London.

I've been acting since I left Manchester University where I was doing Drama and English. I was just reaching the stage where I thought I was going a bit looney – I wanted to be an actress but I didn't think I'd ever be one. I was just one of the community theatre lot, doing cabaret and standup comedy. That's really where I cut my teeth.

I got to my last year at university and I thought, 'I don't know what I'm going to do but I know there are a few things

I want to say'. So I put on a play at the studio, and it all grew from there. The character in the play was me in so many ways. It expressed all the longing of wanting to be an actress and thinking I couldn't be because of where I came from and what I looked like. I didn't have a theatrical family. I didn't know the first thing about getting to be an actress. It was just a silly dream.

All the women I grew up with were marrying pharmacists, having kids and getting a nice house with a garage. Luckily, my parents were unusual in that they were very keen that I should get away from home and learn something. They weren't keen on me acting but, when my dad saw *One of Us*, he was in tears afterwards and said, 'I didn't know you felt like this'. My parents had wanted me to be a doctor or a university lecturer and, in fact, by the fourth year of my university course, I had an MA place, and a year after that I had a teacher's training place and my life was mapped out. *One of Us* broke me out of that. I often think that if it hadn't been so easy for me then, if the show hadn't been taken up and had such a huge success and given me my Equity card, I may well have gone that way.

When I was growing up, I had no role models. Indian women were invisible. I wanted to correct that. I wanted other Indian girls, particularly young people growing up, to see me on television or on the stage and think, 'I do have a place in society. I do have a voice. What I go through is of interest, is of importance'.

Good writing explodes stereotypes. I try and do that. There are expectations, especially when it comes to the Indian community, because everyone has a very fixed idea of what we're like. That's why the first image in *One of Us* is a mad girl on roller-skates wearing a hat with a prawn on it. Everyone knew it was a show about an Indian and they expected someone to come in wearing a sari, with her eyes downcast. Later, you find out that the roller-skates and the hat are the uniform for the restaurant where the girl works. Immediately, you are saying, 'Don't think that way when you look at me'.

That's why theatre is so liberating. It's only in theatre that I've done really challenging and different work which hasn't necessarily been Indian. For TV, everyone is physically stereotyped. If you're overweight, or you have ginger hair or a Scottish accent, you're immediately typecast. You have to try and convince them that as an actress you're versatile. I don't believe in revealing my age – although I wouldn't lie if someone asked me directly – because casting directors are so limited that you can lose a part just because you're a couple of years older than the character. There can be problems, too, if you don't exactly fit the stereotype. My hair is naturally curly and people have often asked me if I'm '100 per cent Indian' because they think all Indian women have straight hair.

In the five years since I started acting in the theatre, I've played an eighteen-year-old, an eighteenth-century Essex village girl who was a deaf mute, and a 35-year-old house-wife. I'd rather do a badly paid fringe play which is expressing something I feel strongly about than carry a spear at the National or the RSC as part of a so-called 'ensemble'. They spin you a yarn about being part of an ensemble, but what happens is that you spear carry from one play to another while star names are drafted in to do the nice juicy roles. Real ensemble acting is when star actors have their fair share of standing around doing nothing, but that doesn't happen. So, in fact, it's largely a myth.

Unfortunately, directors who want bland, unchallenging actresses are not a myth. It's an eternal problem in Britain, and even worse in America. When I was there doing Caryl Churchill's *Serious Money*, there were eight American actors in the cast. All the women were pin thin, absolutely beautiful, manicured, perfectly groomed. They had to be, they said, because 'we are up against the plastic generation, against girls that are eighteen, who go and have nips and tucks and breast implants because they know a bland, pretty face is what gets you places'. They call it the P & G factor: Proctor and Gamble are the people who run all the adverts and the soaps. 'Oh darling, you're not P & G enough' means 'You don't look like anybody in *Dallas*, so you can't advertise this soap powder'. I can see theatre in Britain going that way as the power of the sponsors increases.

I considered staying on in America to try and find work. My American agents were very keen: 'There's nobody like you,' they said. But the competition there is too cut-throat – fame and money seem to be more important than the acting. I feel I've got a niche in Britain. I'm one of the first few British Asian actresses who are making inroads, however small. The work means something.

I've done frivolous work, adverts and training films. Most of the theatre work I've done has been worthy new writing which is probably why nobody knows who I am – I've yet to make it into TV. I'm not considered suitable for the parts for Indian women on television because there aren't Indian women writing for television and the few parts that do exist are written by people who don't know anything about us. They write about nice, pretty, young, slim girls having arranged marriages, or about mums. I'm not everyone's idea of what an Indian woman is. I used to be very overweight. Now I'm much thinner and people look at me very differently, but I have to resign myself to the fact I'm not going to get frequent work.

Actresses who are petite and pretty get all the television work and are hailed as stars. They are taken up to play young girls and at thirty there's no work for them. Then there are the actresses who've been around for a long time, like Anna Massey and Maggie Tyzack, who've done a lot of good work and suddenly flower. That's how I see myself. I'm not going to be a huge flash in the pan. I'm not going to be taken up and sent to Hollywood, but I hope I will still be here in ten years' time, having done a lot of good work, and surviving.

I enjoyed doing *My Girl*, Barrie Keeffe's play at the Theatre Royal, Stratford East, because it was a story about a couple trying to keep their love alive amidst poverty (a reality as far as I'm concerned) and because the part wasn't written for an Asian. I enjoyed it, too, because it's so beautifully written. I also liked doing *Blood* at the Royal Court. I've always enjoyed working there, it's really an actors' theatre. *Blood* was a controversial play which showed the Sikh community in a very uncomplimentary light. People said, 'Oh, the Sikhs aren't going to like this'. We didn't get one complaint from the Sikh community, probably because no Sikhs came to see it. If it had been on TV, it would have been very different. As it was, it was the white liberals who were more frightened of the play than other Indians were. I was playing an Indian woman who landed in England in the 1960s, full of hopes, very ambitious, a strong woman, which is why I liked playing her. Thirty years later, time and broken dreams have taken their toll. I thought, 'God, I've never seen this done before. I know these women, I've got aunties like this who started off as young and beautiful and had a lot of fire and I've seen this society batter it out of them.' It was saying something important. Just to survive is a victory really.

Not that I wish to be too idealistic about being answerable to the Asian community. Most Asians don't know who I am and don't care particularly what I do. They don't think I'm famous unless I've been in *EastEnders*.

When *Sammy and Rosie Get Laid* was on television recently, I certainly didn't tell anybody. I thought, 'I hope to God they don't watch it, me playing a fairly outrageous dyke.' That was Hanif Kureishi just being provocative, but having two very bolshie lesbians in the film, one black and one Asian was like a statement in itself, like actually saying, 'There *are* Asian lesbians. We do exist and we don't take crap'. I see very few films coming out of Britain that are trying to examine what's happening here. Kureishi was putting his politics right on the line.

The only time my acting seems to bother the people I know in the Asian community is when I do something like *Sammy and Rosie*, which is not considered respectable because there's still a stigma about actresses being almost like prostitutes. In India, in the olden days, they were. Still, in India today, it's the people in films who are allowed to have affairs or illegitimate babies, as if they are separate from everyday morality. People accept it. But they would *never* tolerate it next door to them. My mum and dad are very good in that way. They deflect criticism. Now that I'm married to a respectable Indian man, people that would snipe have to keep their mouths shut. Those that do complain about me being an actress probably wouldn't come to see me in something like *Peer Gynt* at the National, anyway.

The only work that I would worry about doing is work that I thought degraded us in any way. I turned down a part in the *Viceroys of India* because somebody was blacking up as Nehru. It would have meant six weeks' work and a lot of money but there's no way I could have done that. You have to draw the line somewhere.

The criteria by which I choose my work are: is it exciting?; is it challenging?; is it truthful? That's more important than whether it's going to be good for the Asian community because the Asian community doesn't really exist. We happen to come from the same part of the world but, like any other group of people, we're completely divided by class, caste, political belief and ambition. There's no way I could please everybody.

Acting is almost a physical need. Being on stage and having that communication with an audience justifies my presence in the world.

The wonderful thing about doing a play is that it's a little piece of life which makes sense. Offstage, it's all a mess and a tangle and you just live it day by day. A play actually puts into perspective some moment of some experience of somebody's life, and you want to share that. When it's a good performance and it goes like a roller-coaster, even if no one comes up to you at the end and says you're wonderful, you know by their response you've contributed something to their emotional life. Nothing can beat that.

I think an actor speaking in a play is more powerful than a hundred political speeches because if someone understands you and if it touches them emotionally, you've opened a lock in their mind more than any rhetoric could. That's the reason I write. Writing is a more cerebral, selfless motive. Although I often write really nice parts for women, I know I'm probably not going to get to play them unless I can wangle it.

A Nice Arrangement was an eleven-minute film, a dialogue between a young Indian girl on the morning of her wedding and a divorcee, which I wrote for Channel 4 with Gurinder Chadha, a documentary film-maker. *Hungry Hearts* was about the growth of the Sikh independence movement in Southall and the Southall Black Sisters women's advice centre which is a little island in the middle of it all. It's still sitting on a shelf. People said to me, 'We're not going to get funding for this, Meera. There are no white faces in it. There's no one we can get that's famous enough to pull in co-funding. Who's going to watch it apart from a few social workers and a few Indians like you?'

I think I'm a pretty optimistic person but every time I'm out of work, I think I'm never going to work again. That's another reason why I've turned to writing. I thought, well, either I go under and I believe that I'm no good or I look at this realistically and understand there are not many parts written for me because of what I look like and who I am. If I sit around waiting for someone to give me a break, it's not going to happen. So I decided to create the work.

Racism is a terrible lesson for a child to learn. I remember when, at school, I cut my finger on a milk-bottle top and all the kids crowded round and said, 'her blood's red, her blood's red'. They couldn't believe it. That was my first inkling that they'd seen me differently. I'm sure that was partly why I became a comedian early on. The way to make friends and stop people picking on me was to make them laugh. It was something people began to admire me for. I also got into a lot of fights. If I got picked on, I just wouldn't take it. I'd hit back. I'm not bitter because, quite frankly, I've been cushioned. I didn't grow up in the East End and have shit pushed through my letter box. My parents always had their own house and, when I was twenty, they moved into a very nice middle-class area near Birmingham. Our neighbours are mostly other professional Indians or nice middle-class white people who, even if they don't like us, are too polite to say so.

If I'd been told at twenty that six years later I'd be at the National, I wouldn't have believed it. Off-Broadway, in *Serious Money*, I thought, 'Now, I could die happy. To be paid, and in New York, for the thing I love most, this is great.' I'm not interested in being a household name. I'd like to be like Maggie Steed, whom I admire enormously, or – dare I say it – Judi Dench. They're not known for being film stars. They can still walk down the street without being recognized but they're tremendously respected. They do important and good work. I'd be happy with that.

The difference between my generation and my parents' is that people of my age feel that having two cultures is a positive advantage. I love being a British Asian. I wouldn't be anything else. I've got the potential for having the best of both worlds. I'm an outsider so I can see both my culture and my host culture more clearly than somebody who grew up in either one. The clash between the two is what gives my work its creative spark.

If I went the thorny way of the soaps, I think I'd find it really hard to get good theatre work. Things are changing but it's still quite a hierarchical system in Britain. This is one thing I like about the Americans. Whether they do soaps, adverts or plays on Broadway, it's work, it's respected and they're not afraid to put it down on their CVs. To a British actor, going into *Howard's Way* is the kiss of death. It shouldn't be. It's TV experience and it pays the rent.

I'd take a running soap if I thought I could stay in it for not more than a year and if it was intelligently written – because they're so powerful. So many people watch *East-Enders*. Soaps could tackle issues such as racism but, unfortunately, they play safe and waste the opportunity. Many of the people who write for *EastEnders* are very good writers but there are some who live in Hampstead and write scripts about the East End when they have only passed through and don't even know any black people. How are they going to write for them with any authenticity or feeling? Of course, white writers *can* write good black parts. As a writer, I'd find it insulting if somebody said I couldn't write a white part. These writers should do their research, but they don't bother.

I finish at the National soon. I don't think I'm going to get anything else there because integrated casting isn't something that happens on a large scale even though the National is changing.

I was offered *Peer Gynt* and Jatinder Verma's *Tartuffe* at the National on the same day. I took *Peer Gynt* because I wanted to work with Declan Donnellan. I do want to work with Jatinder but what put me off was the six-week tour, one- and two-night-stands, and the National's, 'If you're good enough, we'll include you in the repertoire with twelve performances at the Cottesloe'. I didn't like that attitude towards the company. As it turned out, Jatinder's *Tartuffe* was a huge success and I'll probably really regret not being in it. It was quite a difficult choice to make. I did want to work with Declan very badly and I know I'll get to see Jatinder again. However, I've found the Asian connection can also work against me. Hanif Kureishi and Farroukh Dhondy think I'm so utterly successful that I don't need their help.

For the first time in five years I'm thinking: 'I won't write. I won't knock on people's doors. I'm in something at the National, people are going to come and see it. I have a good agent. Let's just see what happens.' It's hard to keep one's skills going because it costs money. I recently did a workshop with Peter Gill on Shakespeare and it left me feeling really unsatisfied because I thought, 'It's so wonderful what you're saying and where am I going to get a chance to do some classical work?'

I think the only way for a black or Asian actress to survive in this profession is to become politicized, with a small 'p'. I've had to justify myself to myself so often about why I'm doing what I'm doing. The only reason that I've hung on and it's made sense is that I know who I am to a certain extent. I can call myself a British Indian person. As a black actress, you have to be more aware because every time you're offered a part, you're thrown back on yourself. What is this part saying? What is it saying about me? What's it saying about the community I come from, or not saying? All the time, you have to think about the justification of yourself as an actress.

There are so few things done about black or Asian people that everything you do immediately becomes representative in people's eyes. If there were five plays on now about the Asian experience, *The Cosby Show*, or whatever about us, then it would be different. Hanif's stuff can be caricatures but I admire him for what he's doing because in the end he says, 'I have to write what I think is truthful' and I say yes to that. That's my bottom line. I probably will do stuff that will offend some people. Too bad. If I've justified it in my own political terms, then I can live with it.

When a young girl comes up to me and says that she wants to be an actress, I say, 'You have to think very carefully about the reality of this profession and what you are going to be asked to do and whether you are up to that, and that's on top of all the other difficulties that every other actor faces. In the end, if you have a burning desire to do it, do it. And you'll be welcomed by the other people here because we want more people.' It's camaraderie cum competition because we're all fighting for the same few crumbs. We see each other at the same auditions all the time even if we're physically different, because we've got brown faces. But if I hear about work that I think somebody else is right for, I do tell them. We have to support each other because, in the end, we're the only people that really understand what it's like.

I suppose I'd be called 'post-feminist' in some ways because I married at twenty-six which would have been a startling idea when I was twenty. I do want children and I'm prepared to juggle them with a career. All that was taboo even when I was at university. The reason I have the confidence to do that is because of the people who went before me in the 1970s and said, whatever your choice, do it with awareness, do it with a sense of self and do it striving for equality. The women in the '70s gave me that choice. I hope that the way I bring up my children will give them those kinds of choices as well.

FIONA SHAW

'Like walking on blades every night'

Born in Cork.

Fiona Shaw already has an impressive number of Shakespeare's leading ladies to her credit with Portia, Beatrice, Kate, Celia, Rosaline and Rosalind. Gold Medal winner at RADA in 1982. Early successes include Mary Shelley in Howard Brenton's *Bloody Poetry* (presented by the excellent but now defunct fringe company Foco Novo), Julia in the National's *The Rivals* – which established her as a superb comedienne – and Celia in Adrian Noble's famous 'whitesheets' version of *As You Like It* with Juliet Stevenson as Rosalind.

Subsequent highlights have included an unforgettable portrayal of Tatiana, the young, unmarried sister in Gorki's *The Philistines* (also RSC), a virtuoso display of comic timing as the dashing Mistress Carol, opposite Alex Jennings in James Shirley's hilarious but fiendishly difficult seventeenth-century comedy of manners, *Hyde Park*, Schiller's tragic heroine Mary Stuart (to Paola Dionisotti's Elizabeth I), Electra in Deborah Warner's RSC production of the same name, and both male and female roles (Shen Te and her male relative Shui Ta) in Brecht's *The Good Person of Sichuan* at the National. She also appeared as the woman doctor opposite Daniel Day Lewis's Christy Brown in the award-winning film *My Left Foot*.

Most recent films include: Bob Rafaelson's *Mountains of the Moon* (about the explorer Sir Richard Burton in which she played Lady Burton), *Three Men and a Little Lady* with Tom Selleck and Ted Danson; and the BBC trilogy *For the Greater Good* by G.F. Newman, about medical research, to be seen in 1991.

She lives in London.

Virginia Woolf was so right when she said that women don't have a country in the same way as men do. Having said that, I get a kind of heebie-jeebies in case that means I'm relinquishing my country. Nationalism is bred with language from the moment you're born. You have a sense of it. Every time I open my mouth, the history of my accent is in my mouth. There's a great myth that the Irish people speak English. We actually don't speak English at all. We use English to appear to be saying the same things that English people are saying but we're not saying the same things. I think that when I live in England I do speak English. When I'm in Ireland I speak in a different idiom.

Being brought up in Ireland means being brought up with a lot of contradictions. I can't even make a statement about my family because there isn't a norm. You can have a very individual upbringing in Ireland because, among other things, it's such a sparsely populated place. Like many Irish families, we're like wild geese – we've been bred for export, really. I've two brothers, both of whom live in the south of France. The third was killed in 1985, just when I went to Stratford. He was only eighteen.

I wasn't consciously bred for export. I went to university in Ireland and studied philosophy at Cork. I was educated within three square miles of myself at a small private school, something quite different to going to a private school in England, I would think. Education is not just to do with schooling. In Ireland, you can't decide who someone is because class isn't as easy to map. The city's so small you know everybody, so there isn't quite the same rigour in terms of strata that you get in England. It's much more subtle.

All this is grist to the mill to an actress because you get to know an awful lot about a lot of things, especially social mannerisms. That got me very interested in the eighteenth century. Restoration plays for some reason tickled me pink because I felt surrounded by Restoration parallels. Access to even older centuries is also all around you in Ireland in ordinary, daily life.

My mother, for example, has a man who comes to deliver milk; in the evening he'll nip up with a bottle. Now, to drive to the house must cost more in petrol money than the price of the milk! There's a kind of attitude that's *completely* different. It is still quite feudal, I suppose, though I didn't realize that until I came to England. Life there isn't just about making money. As with the French, it's about having a lovely time, even when conducting business.

My father comes home every evening from his surgery with endlessly funny stories, slices of life that impinge from the outside world into this tiny microcosm. I think this is the inheritance of any Irish person – just endlessly telling stories. Everybody knows what we're laughing at in Ireland; you don't necessarily know what you're laughing at in England. The playwright Tom Murphy said that the Irish relationship to literature is that, 'we know the subject and we are the subject'. So you're always laughing at yourself *with* yourself. It's incestuous, but it doesn't hurt anyone else except yourself. I think we share more than we don't share. What's so peculiar about England is that people absolutely don't share, the isolation of each grouping is phenomenal.

The other side of it is that I couldn't wait to get out of Ireland. It's a very intrusive society. You're not allowed to have feelings other than the ones you're allowed to have.

Having three brothers, I suppose I felt very much the daughter. I played a part when I first left drama school in *Fireworks for Elspeth* which highlighted that daughtery aspect. That was very me, as I had been before I left Ireland.

I've always wanted to be an actress since I was about seven, although I didn't know what it was to be one. I hardly ever saw a play. I didn't do any plays at school. We used to act things in class sometimes and I did play the judge in Gilbert and Sullivan's *Trial by Jury*. I loved performing. Any instance that I could possibly perform, I'd perform. If there was a dinner at home and people wanted poetry then I'd be down there doing the poetry.

The family is full of performers but I don't think it's particularly unusual – it's the norm in Ireland. My mother sings every evening at the piano, and she holds musical evenings. My brother, Mark, is the actor of the family really! I don't know what I'm doing! He's brilliant, he can make the sound of the bus journey from Galway to Cork including the bus stopping and starting in various towns like Gort! But I wanted to be trained as an actress. I had my eyes firmly set on England rather than Dublin because I was interested in the eighteenth century and English wit. I'd done Lady Wishfor't in *The Way of the World*, and speeches from Wycherley's *The Country Wife*.

So I wrote to RADA, did an audition and got in. I had a brilliant time there. Everything of importance that I learned, I feel, I learned then. Anything that I learned beforehand seems to be sunk unconsciously somewhere, except perhaps some philosophy which helps me see variations of thought, sometimes.

RADA helped me connect my body to my mind. When I first went there, Hugh Crutwell, the principal, said I arrived smelling of libraries! I was only twenty-one, but I felt a fuddy-duddy. He thought he'd have to *drag* me into the twentieth century. I hit the whole punk thing – we hadn't had punk in Ireland. I met completely different types of people here. The youth culture is much harsher in England than in Ireland. And the accents!

I'm more aware about my accent now because people actually seem to mention it to me. For a start, when I went to

RADA, I always played English parts. I can speak standard English but I don't use it for classical roles. Classical acting has become for me about expressing feeling rather than transforming personality.

However, in England, class is really what's revealed through accent. This is a vast and very interesting thing. The English speak in a major key, and the Irish speak in a minor key. In England, language is bright, and it's in G major. The result of that is the English took over the world or vice versa. In Ireland, we have the dying fall. It doesn't mean we are depressed, it just means that we're manoeuvring around language and around our own lives. They are fundamental things, these accents. I had a very privileged education by the standards of either country. But where an Irish accent is concerned, I'm not sure that class doesn't read quicker than country.

A really good comedy is probably the most life-enhancing thing to observe and to be an agent of, because the ability to laugh at ourselves is *profoundly* and singly the most life-saving thing. I'm very keen on the structure of comedy. I just love the way it works, I love the fact that any situation can be funny, just by a twist of the imagination.

In Ireland, I had lived out my life in drawing-rooms where people had a very strict code of behaviour and the moment when it broke I found interesting. The world can end, depending on how you finish a sentence! I used to adore social pretension which is still an endlessly brilliant source of comedy: people attempting to be what they can't be. The failure between their *image* of who they are and who they *are* – the bit in between – for all deliciously sympathetic reasons, is terribly funny, as is people missing each other. Gore Vidal said the tragedy of life is mistiming. I've seen people come in and utter the most awful clangers of sentences. It's fascinating how those vast tidal movements are done in a twist of a word.

There's a wonderful bit at the end of *Antony and Cleopatra* – my favourite line in all of Shakespeare really – when Cleopatra dies, and the soldier comes in, some little thug from Italy, and says to Charmian: 'Charmian, is this well done?' and she says, 'It is well done and fitting for a princess descended of so many royal kings. Ah, soldier!' It feels like the tide goes out all over the world for me when I hear that, 'Ah, soldier'. The combination of those two words says everything Charmian can't even begin to say, and the air in the silent half of the sentence opens a crack in the imagination of the hearer for history and sorrow to fill.

That's why I loved doing *Electra*. I found it very moving to start with someone who's been twelve years grieving. On top of this state is a very precise argument. Her world is so reduced, a bit like Beckett's. There is only one subject. She hasn't gone to university or lived at all. She has only gone in ever shrinking circles. At the moment at which life is so unbearable, it should go into song or opera and it doesn't quite. The emotion ferments and explodes finally, perversely, without any kind of catharsis.

I don't think we could have played it with more intensity or more precisely. There's very little room to manoeuvre, you're just hanging on to the thought on top of this grief. Deborah Warner nearly conducted it, really. It was very hard because it was taking the pinnacle of what you can do with Shakespeare, which is distilling the notion that thought and feeling are the same thing. And there was no relief. I used to dread it as though it was bad for me. I'd stand in a darkened shower, just before the performance, getting ready for the onslaught. But I got to like Electra tremendously. You have to go with her, why she feels so strongly about things – not judge her.

I saw a clip of *Electra* on television. There's a bit where she was throwing herself down on to the circle and so I stopped the machine to see what happened when the body just fell. I was very entertained by it but I felt it was somebody else completely which reminded me that if you take yourself too seriously, you're lost.

Very few actors really feel the emotions. We perceive things at about six different levels at one time. I can be playing Electra and knowing that I'm down on this little bit there even whilst doing it. You're lifting things and adjusting, whilst absolutely being in it at the same time. That's how self-conscious we are as people.

Every now and then though, actors play a part that really says something about who they are. I went into acting because of comedy so I was very surprised that Electra seemed to be the thing that was much nearer who *I* was when I played it.

I always told myself I could do tragedy. That's why I didn't have any interest in doing it, because, I thought, 'I know what it is; it's about being very upset, making yourself very unhappy'. Comedy interested me much more. But, of course, I'm avoiding something.

I think tragedy is expensive. After the *Electra* run, I was in a terrible state for many months, utterly worn out. I went walking in Greece to try and recover. I didn't realize it was going to be like that. I was very depressed and upset, like going to the moon – it's very hard to know what has meaning afterwards.

What interested me about the whole experience was that this play, after 2,000 years, got an audience to grieve in some way in a country that has lost almost all ritual of grief.

Literature, I think, is humanity's dialogue with itself and an actor is the interpreter of the text of the *writer*, who is tapping the soul of who we all are. The best one does is to give it expression – the key being one's own grief that reveals a very dark pool of basic grief that everybody has. The actor allows it out specifically in the moment. In the end, I suspect, that dark pool is a very similar pool to everybody else's pool.

I don't think I can claim we're high priests or priestesses for putting anybody back in touch with anything, but sometimes we do and, more than sometimes, it's what we should try to do. I think people want to be put back in touch with a bit of themselves that is not culturally connected to who's currently prime minister. We're so told who we are at the moment. That's what we're trying to escape in the theatre but it's actually a return – an attempt to return to a state where time passes through us rather than us through time. Plays do that where there's an infusion of the imagination and other realities. In those worlds you're always freer than you are in our horrid world of urban councils. Ibsen is the great urban council writer!

Brecht, of course, is another thing entirely. He has irony of situation rather than irony of language. *The Good Person of Sichuan* is an epic which was very satisfying to do but it's a taxing role and I did do my voice in.

I played the dual role of Shui Ta and Shen Te. When I played Shui Ta, the male relative of Shen Te, the change of voice caused havoc with my vocal chords. As long as I was talking down low I was all right, but as soon as I got up high they couldn't do it. It was like walking on blades every night and expecting to be a runner. Lunacy.

I liked playing Shui Ta. I thought he was sexy because he was powerful. I played him a whole lot of different ways. I changed him into different characters I'd seen on television. If I didn't do some vocal twisting, I didn't have fun. I have to have fun. Fun is nearly always danger. I was a great one in Stratford for staying up all night and then doing a matinée. Silly, I think it's exhausted me now!

I was so excited about going to Stratford because it was like going to Oxford or Cambridge. You were going 'up' to Stratford. I remember seeing a photograph of Janet Suzman on the front of *Plays and Players* in Cork playing Cleopatra. I thought, there's a breed of people who must have been bred to be this thing called an actress. Janet Suzman was obviously one of them. It seemed so inaccessible. So to be asked to go to Stratford was like being allowed into the garden of a great house and playing with the toys! I could have died thereafter. Every day I used to wake up very excited, with a bubble in my stomach.

That first year was one of the few experiences in my life which lived up to its expectations totally. I met a whole lot of people who seemed to be like minds to myself and, I think, like a lot of over-protected people, I function well in an institution – particularly reacting against it, but happy to be in it rather than the free-lance world where being streetwise, which I'm not at all, is important.

On the small-scale tours, where I did Portia and Beatrice with Nigel Terry, my Shakespeare training really took off. I saw it all as a learning experience, and I don't mean that crudely. I've always felt that you have to stay at something to get any good at it. There's a real instant culture we're in at the moment and it's not really the thing.

The good thing about playing the classics I find is that I use muscles I wouldn't use in a lot of modern playwriting. The joy of playing these vast roles is that you get a chance to expand who you might be, including very contradictory and often unattractive aspects of who one is – because one wants to be that too!

There is a remarkable difference between being the person who is supporting and the person who is carrying the burden of the evening. Very often, the supporting role seems more difficult because you're injecting suddenly, like a turbo engine. You come in and have to serve the rhythm that has already been set in the piece whereas a leading character can warm up in the evening. That's the theory.

In fact, you can't. If you're the leading character you've got to come in and *be* it, although you have more room to manoeuvre if you go a bit wrong. If you're the support, you've got to make your statement much more clearly and, of course, the better the writing, the more interesting the supporting character often is.

Celia in *As You Like It* is one of the best written roles *ever*. What's extraordinary is that she can do so much in such a short time. Compared to the amount of speech that Rosalind has, Celia's impact is enormous. The great joy for me in playing Celia was not having to carry the evening, so the room to also create the character more laterally was there. Anna Massey once said that whenever she's reading a part in which she's meant to be playing the maid, she always assumes that the play is about the maid! It's wise to assume that one's world is about oneself. And that's enhanced if you're playing a kind of egocentric like Celia. The discovery the first time I did the play was quite extraordinary. It was the play in which I fell through the looking glass in relation to Shakespeare. I fell so in love with that play, I would have loved to have made a film of it but I realized in one way it is the 'play of plays'. You should never make a film of it because it is as individual as one's dreams.

Adrian Noble directed the Stratford production with a firm hand. Big theatre productions include the constraint of a predetermined set. I think it's no bad thing to have a constraint. You've got to start somewhere. You have to get on and do the play. Adrian allowed us to go quite far on that play because it is the most anarchic world once you get to Arden. It is somewhere in the inside of the brain. I think we all went kind of mad, really, with what we thought it was. That one got known as the 'white sheets' version.

Part of the problem for the two women in that play, as in many of Shakespeare's plays, is that they have no mother. The absence of mothers always puts women in a state of crisis from the start. They are unprotected, they are always alone in the world, even if the world is a drawing-room.

I like having my dressing room crowded with people at the 'half'. I'm better when I've been distracted up to the last minute. Some people absolutely need calm and peace. I don't, because being on the stage to me is not dissimilar to being in life. It doesn't mean I'm acting all the time. On the contrary. But far from resting your voice before a performance, I think you should use it. It is, after all a machine and needs to be kept well oiled.

I truly think that as much as you need imagination to act you also need a really big failure of imagination as well. To get on stage, you have to numb your imagination. Stage fright is the sudden realization of what you are doing – stage fright is sanity to the point of misery because somewhere you expose yourself.

Acting is a mixture – it can be a cover as well as a revelation. As in life, one can choose to reveal or to hide oneself, so the stage is the same. I prefer not to play that life game. I hide behind the lack of glamour. If I wanted you to see me, I'd glam up a bit. That's my cover. I don't want to be judged for my appearance – unless I choose to be judged for that. So, say, if I play Electra, I cut my hair or starve myself – or, for Shen Te, I made sure she was the plainest woman in the village. One's vanity is perverse, really.

It works for me not being too protective of whatever attributes I have. They become malleable, depending on the role. There's no point trying to be sexy as Electra, for example, but there is an appeal, whether it's sex appeal or communication appeal. There's personality appeal, I think, in the vibrancy of a mind. Passion is itself appealing, or isn't – but if it is, then to those it is, it is.

I also think there's a beauty in being ugly and in not being fearful of being ugly. There's a beauty in being true. People are often very beautiful when they radiate a truth. When it comes to dealing with 1,500 people looking at me, though, personal vanity has to go. You have to just pick someone in the audience and play the play as though it is a dialogue with them.

Parents are another thing. In *Mephisto* I had to lift up my skirt and show my totality and I saw my parents in the stalls as I did it, and a thought went through my head about these people who were the genetic formula that produced *this* genetic lump. I saw them look at me and I felt so sad because I thought, 'What have they done to produce this genetic lump that is now throwing back at them this genetic lump or combination?' It's very odd having your parents in, there's something very profound at play there.

Without being wishy-washy liberal, I do think male and female directors each have their own advantages, although it's very hard to find out what the differences are without them appearing to be qualitative. Deborah Warner has the ability of not appearing to make her ego an agent in the room. The fact is, she's the tightest rein that you're likely to come across but you don't feel that initially. Adrian Noble's intellect is so ranging it's terribly exciting to be around, very clever and brave – real boy-brave.

Women obviously can get blocked somewhere. The women directors who are successful are very successful. It's in the middle range that we need more of them, although it's not really fair to dump that problem just on to the theatre.

137

It's the world generally. My skin starts to crawl because if you become too aware of the imbalance you become so dominated by it that it takes away your power to overcome it. I can't surmount the fact that 98 per cent of professors are men. When you face that head on, it's just unspeakable. So I have to build a tunnel to get through it. But there are also other things like the thing about the piece of cake and whether we want the same recipe.

There is a lot perhaps in women's character, or cultural character, which women must develop. You've to become bigger as a woman. Women must opt to be big, and the cost of that is you may be less popular as a woman. It is very difficult, but there's only so far backwards one can bend.

Of course, success is a great protector from everything. I've been very lucky, I have played probably three of the biggest parts for men or women, bar Hamlet, on the stage this year.

I was asked to play Hamlet recently. I'd love to play it if it released anything – again, it's to do with the size because he's some sort of western European consciousness. Whether a woman could bring anything to it, I don't know.

Taming of The Shrew, which I did with Jonathan Miller, was a real quest. I was trying to protect Katharina and the psychological end-result of his decision about her. He decided very early on that she was damaged, that she was behaving badly because she was unloved. I took that as far as it could go. What happens to women who feel damaged? They tend to damage themselves.

There was also the fact that there's a breakdown of language at the beginning of the play. Petruchio has all the lines. This woman, who is so eloquent at the end of the play, has no language at the beginning, she doesn't even speak great truths about the community. I thought, 'Well maybe she *can't* express herself because the same woman *can* so eloquently at the end of the play.' So she damages herself, like many women and the Irish themselves. She doesn't damage anybody else.

You have to believe these women are real people because you're making pictures out of yourself, you're turning yourself into something just by suggestion to yourself. But if you can't suggest it, you can't do it. The things you have to do as them are so not like yourself. Being them well, being them very fully, is what's so difficult. Directors sometimes, too, are frights for asking one to play abstractions. I was once asked to play a character and they said 'she is Ireland'. You can't play Ireland, you can only play Molly Malone or Kathleen ni Houlihan.

Working in film is very different; it's like archery, you're just hitting the same bull's-eye every time. Your success is in knowing you've just made something happen that might just get mapped on to celluloid. It's quite an interesting, intense kind of joy. Just for a moment, you get something right and very few people will have noticed you've got it right – the director, maybe the cameraman will, and then the audience eventually. It's a peculiar kind of buzz really.

When you communicate fun across celluloid, that's a good thing. Relaxation is difficult because it's a very tense medium whereas, at its best, the stage creates a sort of relaxed playground; it's a freeing place. Great film actors would also say that film is very free. The more I do, the more I find that is so.

Jonathan Miller told me this great story about an ambitious young man, who, when asked what he was going to do said, 'Well I'm hoping to want to be an architect'. You have to *want* to do it, be an actress, not *hope* to want to do it!

I don't know how long I will do it, I hate to think that my three score years and ten will be taken up with being an actress. I am very much not an actress when I'm not acting. But you do become it. Being an actress becomes a way of life. I am not someone who *wants* to be an actress, I am one.

MAUREEN LIPMAN

'Comedians make it look easy'

Born Hull, LAMDA trained.

Maureen Lipman is one of our wittiest actresses, with a wicked line in gangly, slightly off-centre characters (her recent metamorphosis into Beattie, British Telecom's archetypal Jewish mother, could be said to be yet a further extension of this). She has spent seasons with both the National and the RSC but it is for her television and West End work that she is best known, in plays by Ayckbourn, Richard Harris, Alan Plater, Alan Bennett and her husband, Jack Rosenthal; and in the award-winning TV series, *Agony* and *All At Number 20* (for which she won the *TV Times* Funniest Female award).

On stage, the wise-cracking, effervescing Ruth of Leonard Bernstein's musical, *Wonderful Town*, seemed positively written for her (and, not surprisingly, won her the Variety Club of Great Britain award). Her rubber-legged Miss Skillen in the Ray Cooney farce *See How They Run* also won her both an Olivier and Variety Club award in 1984.

She has also appeared in darker-toned plays, notably Martin Sherman's *Messiah*, and Central TV's *About Face*, which gave her multifaceted gifts even wider scope; 'achingly funny scripts . . . above all due to Miss Lipman's dazzling talent, given free rein here in a series of completely different central roles' (Noel Malcolm, *Daily Telegraph*).

More comic restraint – and acute observation – was also to be found in her funny and touching one-woman show *Re: Joyce*, based on the life and work of Joyce Grenfell, which she also took to the Long Wharf Theatre in Connecticut.

Film: major role in *Up the Junction* and cameo in Willy Russell's *Educating Rita* (with Michael Caine).

She has published two bestselling books – *How Was It For You* and *Something to Fall Back On*; and has a regular magazine column.

She is married to writer Jack Rosenthal. They have two children and live in London.

142

I don't believe in the myth of Jewish humour as such, because people are either humorous or they're not. Three per cent of America is Jewish, but eighty per cent of American-humour is Jewish, so, how do you explain it?

I don't think there is a specifically Jewish humour, it's really more Middle European. If you believe as I do that most humour springs out of pain, then it's perfectly obvious why people with a Middle-European background tend to make light of life. Otherwise, they would spend most of it in tears. Whether you appreciate what's known as Jewish humour, whether you find Jackie Mason funny, is another kettle of croissants.

So-called Jewish humour is really metropolitan, city humour, where things are tough. Liverpudlians are renowned for their humour. It's the same thing – where you get a mixed ethnic group and a lot of poverty. Let's be honest, there's not an enormous amount of humour comes out of the aristocracy. When did you read *The Aristocrat's Book of the Biggest Jokes in the World!?* Noël Coward was working class, wasn't he? The death of sitcom is precisely because of that. Television humour is almost entirely middle class. Not since Johnny Speight has there been a writer who's really catering for blue collar workers.

My mother is naturally funny, in a very Gracie Allen manner. She doesn't know she's funny. I mean she can laugh at a joke if it's a certain type of joke. She's very good company but she'll never understand why we all spend most of the time with her falling on the ground. The other day in the kitchen, she said, 'I'm going to get some shin and bone for some soup', and I said, 'No don't get beef at the moment, I don't like this whole thing with the mad cow disease'. She said, 'Oh, well I'll get lamb chops then' – pause – 'is that beef?' What do you say?

A friend of mine said, 'You know the main thing about

your mother's being so funny is because she's got a funny voice', and she does have a funny voice. It's got that kind of American dumb blonde in it.

I took my mother to the National Gallery and, as we walked into that incredible foyer with all the pictures and everything around it, she stood there for exactly the right period of time to make the timing perfect, and then said 'Are these all pictures?'! She is the mistress of the rhetorical question, and it's quite mind-boggling because your only answer can be, 'No, they're rhinoceri'. You don't want to be rude, and it's partly to do with that very northern-ness and that wonderful innocence. Sometimes I think it's not innocence at all. Sometimes I think it's deeply malicious. But most of the time I think it's just a very ingenuous need to be reassured that what she knows to be true is true.

My dad was a witty, sarcastic and somewhat cynical man and he was well known among those in Hull who knew him – he had a tailor's shop – for letting the odd comment drip out of the side of his mouth. He was a sort of northern Coral Browne, if you like. Towards the last fourteen years of his life, he lost his memory after having an operation. He was still endearing and funny but it was never the same old Maurice.

My brother is clever and also very funny, although I probably didn't think so as a child; we fought like cat and Rottweiler. He was very much the wit of his class, a Geoff-the-Lad. Now we adore each other's company and enjoy each other's quick wit.

Some of my mother's family are in America and were part of a Russian dance troupe called the Boris Fridkin troupe. They dressed extraordinarily in these Russian Tsarist-type clothes. There's quite a strain of that sort of performing in the family.

On my father's side, I don't know of anything theatrical,

but there were about eight kids. It was like *Rambo* in that house. So that was the background – a lot of laughter. It was all very much to do with sparking off, and not very far from abrasive, particularly among my father's brothers and sisters.

I was one of those performing children, which rather alienated my brother from me. I sang and did imitations and was very much pushed by my mother to perform. I don't suppose anybody ever thought I'd actually go on the stage. I certainly didn't look like a stage child. I was quite plain and mousey-looking with protruding teeth, whereas my mother is a very beautiful woman. She would have loved to be an actress but she doesn't have any of the qualities that are needed for it. She's deeply self-conscious when she is interviewed or asked questions and goes completely and prettily pink.

I didn't need much pushing. I was always the first kid on stage at the pantomime. When they said, 'Are there any little children who would like to' – vroom, I was up there.

At school, I did the normal school plays. I was very successful in a production of *Dr Faustus* in which I played Faustus, but the next term I was down to playing Dogberry, much to my disgust. I had my nose put out of joint for a while. Anyway, I took elocution lessons, did all the musical festivals and, after A Levels, went to drama school.

I got into LAMDA which was the second place I'd been interviewed by. The first place was Rose Bruford and they turned me down. Now I look back and have sat in on some myself, I realize that I did very unusual audition pieces. I pieced together a series of speeches from Thornton Wilder's *Our Town* and added a lot of mime which I've always been interested in. I was quite big, not that I'm tall, but I was well built in those days. I think they probably thought I would make a good character actress. You always need one person like that at drama school, someone who's got a bit of weight.

I stayed there for two and a half years and enjoyed it very

much. I learned to live away from home, the value of a five pound note in the Earls Court Road, and how to speak to men – which I didn't know much about – and learned to use my humour in order to get myself out of situations when I spoke to the wrong men.

Then I got my first job at the Watford Palace, which was by dint of a trick. (I beg you to look in my book to see what it is, because, it's not that it's such a good trick, it's just that I can't bear to tell you about it again!) My second job was also a trick, when I got the film of *Up the Junction* (and that's also written down), and then after that I played mostly comedy.

I've never really hankered after classical parts. Only with Maggie Smith do I ever feel it's possible to be totally naturalistic in Shakespeare. I never sit there, like I might do in a modern play and go, 'Christ, why does Felicity Kendal always get those parts?'

I did do *Love's Labour's Lost* with Elijah Moshinsky and I truly enjoyed that because he did it very naturalistically. I never felt that I had to think about verse and line and iambic pentameter and anything other than 'I am this sort of person' and 'I want that from that sort of person'. I don't think that I couldn't do it, in fact I know that I probably could. It's just that I don't hanker after it, and I know that there are a lot of people who do it better than me.

Then, again, there's always this in the classics, they invariably will dig up some comedian like Bill Maynard, when he was alive, or Jim Dale, and slap 'em in a Shake-speare with Thora Hird and say, 'My god, these people can really act!' Yes, of course they can act! What do you think we're doing? Do you think it's so easy to gauge the laughs every night with a different house and twenty-five Japanese businessmen in the front row? You think that's not acting, when you suspend a pause, you suspend timing? It's hard. But the argument about comedy over tragedy is endless.

Comedians make it look easy – good ones do. Tragedians make it look hard. When I was doing *Re: Joyce* over in America, a friend of mine who's a voice coach said to me, 'You know, you make it look easy and that won't do in this country'. By the end, I could feel the electricity in the house. It was like a party, like being one person with the audience. Yet it was a very poignant ending, not funny at all. Maybe because of that, the audience never got up on their feet and applauded as I've sometimes seen them do for one-man shows. I didn't think it was because they didn't appreciate it. This chap said, 'When Judy Garland wanted to hit a top note, she pointed at the ceiling. She put her head down and took a deep breath, and she told them in that gesture that she was gonna hit that note. Then she hit it. And then she told them she'd hit it!'

Tell 'em what you're gonna do, do it, and then tell 'em you've done it – it's the old rule of comedy. They go wild then and think you're wonderful because they're in on the secret. It's like when actors corpse on stage. As long as the audience know why they're corpsing, they love it. If you say something funny, that's even better.

I remember the night when a drunken Dane was in the audience in *Re: Joyce*. I was doing the audition piece, 'Is anybody out there'? He stood up and said, 'Yes, I'm here!' I said, very Joyce-like, 'I don't know who you are, but you've stood up before in one of my sketches. Now, the next time you get the urge to do it, kindly don't!' He sat down and the audience gave me a round of applause.

When I was at the Long Wharf in Newhaven, Connecticut, a huge object fell just when I was talking about magic. I was saying something like, 'Magic to me does not mean abracada-bra and fairy godmothers, it means certain –' when bang! this huge spotlight fell down. I said, 'It means certain moments when large objects crash to the ground and you have to pretend nothing's happened.' The audience loved it.

I watched *Steel Magnolias* the other night. I took Amy, my daughter, and I thought at least we'd have a good cry, if nothing else. When the daughter had died, the moment came when somebody said, 'Shelby would have loved that', and the mother said, 'Yep, she would have been in the pink'. Because we all knew that Shelby was married in pink and she loved pink, there was a little poignant moment from the script which is probably 'uh, pink'. It wasn't enough for Sally Field, who's a very good actress but very much prone to demonstrating all her emotions. She had to have a moment and say, meaningfully . . . 'pink'.

Now, that is manipulating emotions. I don't want to have anything to do with that. Restraint is the most attractive quality! Of course, there are going to be nights when you're not going to feel the emotions that are necessary but, if you get into pulling those strings, if you move into that category of 'this is the moment when I make them open the purse and take out a hankie', then you're guilty of massive over-indulgence. We've all been guilty of it. There are nights certainly when I've done it – but I never set out to do it. An awful lot of people do, and it's so obvious.

There was a lot of pathos in the second half of *Re: Joyce* but that was entirely to do with Joyce's own Christian Science beliefs and just trying to show the truth of those, and her own, wonderful philosophy about humour and about performing.

When Joyce Grenfell first went into the theatre she was an amateur and she said she was aware that an awful lot of professional actors regarded the audience as a sort of hostile beast that had to be tamed and brought round to love them. She couldn't understand that because she talked to her Christian Science practitioner who said, 'There is no giving without receiving. I put out my hand, but unless you put out yours to receive it, there is no completed action.' So Joyce went out and loved her audience, and they loved her back, which didn't mean to say there weren't some nights when she was awful, and some nights when they weren't awful. I'm sure she came off as I do saying, 'Lord, what a dreadful lot tonight'. But you know those are the nights that surprise you when you say, 'I don't believe this audience, they have got to be morons from another planet', and then somebody will be in that night and they'll come round and say, 'God, it was wonderful' or 'I did love the bit about so and so'. And you have to give up your paranoia.

The big thing to remember with a comedy – and you always forget it, no matter how bright you are – is that the audience who are in tonight were not in last night. They don't know that there's normally a laugh there. You get one laugh, two laughs and you don't get the third laugh, and you begin to think, 'They hate me, they don't like me, they're not going to laugh at the next one', and then of course they don't, because you're thinking about the laugh rather than about what you're saying.

There's a wonderful Alfred Lunt story where he had a line which was 'Can I have a cup of tea' and he always got a laugh on it. One night he just didn't get the laugh and he never got it again! He did it fast and he did it slow, he did it loud and he did it soft, and finally in desperation he said to Lynn Fontanne, 'I don't understand why I don't get that laugh these days on "Could I have a cup of tea".' She said, 'Perhaps, darling, if you tried asking for a cup of tea instead of asking for a laugh you might get it back.'

I met a marvellous lady called Carolyn Heilbrun in a forum I did in America. Her book, *Writing Women's Lives*, shows how women writers, like George Sand and George Eliot, had to reinvent their lives in order to write because ambition was unfeminine. At the forum, she made the point about the way Joyce Grenfell had gone into the business. The story goes that she did a sketch at a party and Herbert Farjeon came up to her and said, 'I want you to do that in my revue' – and that's how she got started.

Carolyn Heilbrun, quite rightly as it's turned out, said, 'Joyce had to reinvent that story, it seems to me, because it was important to her age and class not to be regarded as someone who was going to go in to show business; it was *totally* against the Astor background and the Christian Science and everything else, which is all to do with lack of self.'

Carolyn was right. We all do this self-deprecating thing, I've done it already here: 'Well I got my first job through a trick, I got my second job through a trick and then other jobs followed'; or 'I was plain, I wasn't the sort of person who would go in to . . .'. It's not seemly to say, 'I wanted to be a big success. I knew I had talent, I set out to do it. If I've hurt anybody along the way, then I probably have, and I probably meant to.' It's not nice. Nobody wants to hear about it.

When I stood up as a child and performed, and sang 'You dreamboat, you lovable dreamboat' and my mother shouted at me to roll my eyes when I sang it and 'don't forget the laugh in your voice' – at the same time as I was being encouraged to do that, there was always someone in the room who was sitting there thinking, 'Tch, I wouldn't let a child of *mine* perform like that', as indeed I would think now, if my own children did it.

That is one side of the coin, but I think it's the same side as the sense memory that women all have about not pushing forward. It's not nice, and certainly in Britain it's not nice. Let them come to you. Of course, my whole thing about actors is that I love the ones who make you go to them. It's all part of that sense memory which goes, 'Ah, ah, ah, ah, a little restraint here' and, as far as women are concerned, is the great thing that holds us back because, to achieve what we want to achieve, we've had to use ambition, determination, maybe selfishness and blood on the lino to get there. All those negative emotions, all those chameleon qualities that you use shamelessly in order to get what you want, are not regarded as feminine or even likeable traits in a human being. They're not even regarded as nice in politicians or in businessmen. But you can't get anywhere without them.

The fact that I have always been able, because of this sixth sense, to present what I think is needed meant I often got the job. It also meant that few people ever saw the real me. I was offered the *Wogan* show a little while ago, to take over while he was away. I told the producer I couldn't do it. He said, 'But you'd be brilliant, you'd be perfect.' I said, 'Yeah but it'll give me an ulcer. It's not what I *do*.' I'm an actress and because I have this quality to be able to be quick-witted, it means that I'm in the front line for being a personality. I give off that impression, but it's not always what I want.

The fact is, I also use a lot of my own life. I don't sit down and write it, but everybody knows that there's a large chunk of Maureen Lipman in most of the things that I do on chat shows and interviews. Now, as an actress, I seek not to do that. That's why I hate sitcom so much, because it's totally reliant on the personality of the artist who is performing it. I'm trying all the time to submerge my own personality into that of the character.

You don't watch Lucille Ball to see somebody else. People will say, 'That Penelope Keith, I love it when she does Margot.' But when she tried to play a woman having an affair with a young man – a toy-boy – they didn't want to know. I don't care whether they want to know or not. So I do something like my last series, *About Face*. The ideas for most of the plays were my own and I worked with the director for *months* in pre-preparation for all those different characters. I wanted – especially in the light of British Telecom which has labelled me somewhat – to do what I think I do best, which is to be versatile and to show that I can bury myself in six different women. So that's precisely what we did and I was very pleased with it and *proud* of it. When I left the country, I thought I'd left a good series behind.

When the people from Central TV flew to America to see me, it was like being told at the end of a school year that your work was good, but not good enough. They said, 'People didn't understand what it was. What was it? Were you being one thing, were you being another? They'd just got used to you in one role. There's got to be a concept here.' Why? And whose concept? When the British Academy of Film and Television Arts (BAFTA) awards came out, it was entered as *six different plays*, not a series. Even the makeup, which was brilliant, didn't get on the list. Who's deciding what popular appeal is? The lowest common denominator is deciding. It's the shock of the new because first series are never accepted.

It won't stop me pushing into new areas but it might stop other people from allowing me to because, if they don't get the figures, then the network don't want to know about them. It's all to do with the ratings, with ITV companies all squabbling for slots.

They want you to do what you always do. After twenty-five years, I don't think I've ever played the same part except once in a play called *Outside Edge*, a smashing play by Richard Harris and a very funny character. She was very working class and she'd got this little husband she was deeply devoted to, particularly sexually. She was a bricklayer and everybody loved this woman. In a TV movie some time later, a terrible version of *St Trinians*, I played a private detective and I was so in love with the character, this large, overbearing but strangely sexy woman, that I used it again.

Apart from that I've never done the same thing twice. Then along comes British Telecom and I'm a Yiddisher momma! Twenty-five years goes out the window!

I don't think Beattie in the advertisements is a stereotype. They just reflect one particular person irrespective of class, creed or religion. Actually, she could be Italian or Chinese or whatever. If sharing a recognition of a truth is called being a stereotype then, all right, you could say she is a stereotype and every character that we play truthfully could be called a stereotype.

As for the popularity of mother-in-law jokes and jokes about women generally, I think it's because women were at home all the time. You get used to them being there, like an old pair of slippers or the kitchen wallpaper. Now, with fathers, people tend to write *plays* about them, rather than jokes – maybe because fathers are not always at home, so they're viewed more objectively.

Why do we always try to analyse humour? Why don't we analyse anger or hate? It's all part of the human personality. I happen to think people are funny and humour is one of the things that makes us different from other animals. I don't think it's a question of picking out one race, creed or religion. We're all funny. Humour is just one way of getting a view of ourselves. There are a lot of WASP jokes, for example, in America, and jokes in Canada about Newfoundland. There's always got to be some scapegoat. We use humour as a kind of release.

Before Beattie, I'd never done a commercial. But I thought to myself, 'This is a nest egg'. How else does an actress ever earn any money if she doesn't do films – and I never do. In twenty years, I've never had a film interview. It just never happens. Maybe I don't have a film face. One of the regrets I have, although I don't think it's too late, is that I don't do more of the *Whose Line Is It Anyway*, standup, alternative kind of comedy. I used to do it because I like modern things. I'm not a period person at all. Put me in a cloche hat in *Poirot* and I would just look absurd. So I thought, 'Here I've got this commercial. If I've got a nest egg behind me, I'll be able to do six months on the fringe if I want to.' So that's what I took it for.

I don't write the ads but I put in my two penn'orth. A lot of the end lines are mine. The 'ology' commercial as it stood was entirely Richard Phillips – who usually writes them and now directs them as well – until the bit at the end about 'teachers, a lot of them can't mark, a lot of them can't see', which is just me rambling on. He always lets me do that.

I was at a Royal Film Performance the other night, and the man who was with the Duke of Edinburgh said, 'This is Maureen Lipman, she works for British Telecom'. So, finally, after twenty-five years they have managed to do what I've always avoided – pigeon-hole me.

It's had a huge effect on my career. Every one of the *About Faces* was described as 'Beattie doing flamenco', 'Beattie' trying this or that. Curiously enough, it doesn't hurt, because I know that they are good, and they're hugely successful. But it frightens me in terms of the future because I know that I was on a certain trail and I was just bobbing along nicely. *Re: Joyce* was wonderfully successful and the series was happening.

Then I realized, I have to accept this because Beattie is on TV all the time. If you're on every day you've got to take what comes with it, good and bad. You've got to take people in the street saying, 'Where's your son Melvin?', and you've got to smile and you've got to like it, because you knew what you were doing when you took the job, and if you didn't, it was your own fault. You've become a mother-in-law joke!

If I were a director and I was making a *cinéma vérité* TV movie about some woman who was tall and dark and angular and led a peculiar life in some way, and the casting director said, 'Oh what about Maureen Lipman', I would say, 'Oh no, she's too well known as Beattie'. On the plus side, I like the ads. I have fun making them and sometimes they even make me laugh. I have nothing against them except that they have closed some options, for the time being. The lady who did the Oxo adverts, she never worked for fifteen years! She's still crumbling somewhere.

I look at it in a more sanguine way now because I write as well, and I think, if the acting stops tomorrow, if nobody wants me, it really doesn't matter. I've got a life, I can write articles. Even when you're famous, or you've got a high profile, you know it's all going to change, you're only famous for five minutes.

Re: Joyce is the happiest thing I've ever done. It's hard concentrating if you're not feeling up to it but at least you're not having to rely on anyone, there's no one else to worry about – just me and Dennis King, my pianist, and we get on well. There is something terrific about being your own boss and not having anyone to answer to, as long as you've got a good, strong director, which I had with Alan Strachan.

The reaction to *Joyce* was better in America than in Britain. I don't exactly know why that should be. It was brighter and better. Maybe partly because we were playing it in the round, well three-quarters in the round. So the whole thing was like a party. The Americans brought no preconceptions to it, either of me or of Joyce. In Britain, it took a good ten minutes to get over the barrier and then a lot of manoeuvring around to say, 'I'm not gonna mock her', 'I'm not gonna be rude about her', 'I'm not gonna do an impersonation of her'. In America, they knew nothing and, within five minutes, they were into it. They could stand back and be objective about her.

Joyce and I are awfully similar in a lot of ways. Not

spiritually, and not in our way of life. She was a total original but an aristocrat basically, and I don't know anybody like that. The similarity is in what we do, the manner in which we do it and the way we approach a character. Lots of her friends say, 'it's just uncanny', but it's not even that. It's something to do with watching people and knowing certain things intuitively, the humour and the bossiness and the slight not suffering of fools gladly. She had such an acid but truthful eye for observing people – wicked but never cruel. Alan Bennett and Victoria Wood have to take their hats off to Joyce.

Spiritually, it's the most enchanting time I've had in the theatre, ever. I really did ring Michael Codron after one night at the Vaudeville Theatre and say, 'I want you to put one of those notices outside saying, 'The happiest evening I've ever spent in the British theatre – Maureen'. It's true. I just love it. When it works – as with *Re: Joyce* – it's sheer bloody magic.

SUE JOHNSTON

*'I'm a bit of a perfectionist,
as much as you can be in a soap'*

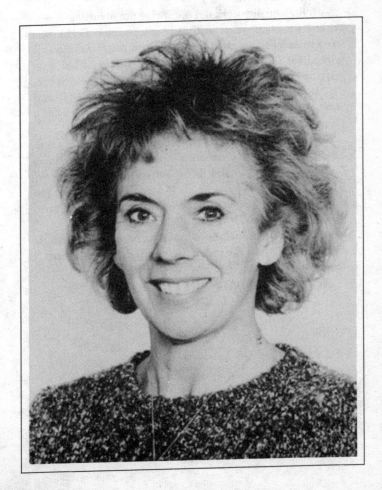

Born Warrington. Trained Webber Douglas School.

A hugely popular actress who, as Sheila Grant in *Brookside*, Channel 4's Liverpool soap, attained something akin to folk heroine status, for a number of years making the eight o'clock slot compulsive twice-weekly viewing.

Radiating a remarkable emotional truth, Sue Johnston's performances – and she would say, thanks to the scripts that produced them – were proof positive that popular television need not necessarily be synonymous with second best or a lowering of standards.

Such high-quality work did not spring out of nowhere. Sue worked for many years in theatre-in-education (TIE). She was a founder member of the north-west company, M6 and worked for some time with Coventry TIE, one of the most respected in the country. She worked with Portable Theatre, the company founded by Howard Brenton, David Hare and Snoo Wilson in the early seventies, where she appeared in David Hare's *Slag* and his version of Genet's *The Maids*.

She has also appeared at Contact Theatre in Manchester in Edward Albee's *A Delicate Balance* and Dario Fo's *Accidental Death of an Anarchist*, and has spent seasons at the Library Theatre, Manchester and at the Bolton Octagon where Jim Cartwright's *To* first originated – the play she brought to London with actor John McCardle.

Television work includes *Coronation Street*, and *Drink the Mercury* (BBC2); on the radio, narrator for the BBC1 series *A Certain Age*.

She lives just outside Liverpool with her son.

When I started, we didn't know *Brookside* was going to be a soap. It was just going to be a serial. Soaps weren't such a phenomenon then. Every day, as you did it, it seemed just a job and then, every so often, it'd catch you up. You'd walk down the street or do a charity and you'd get mobbed. Then you'd think, 'Oh, this is to do with the television' and, actually, you don't have to be a good actress or actor to get that. That's the power of television. You only have to be on it. It in no way says that you are good at your job. It just means you're on the television and that carries a lot of weight with people.

I learned to accept it – the acclaim – but, to be honest, I didn't like it because to me it was just a job, one that I was always struggling to do well. I have high standards about my work, even if it is only a soap to some people. There were times when I knew I wasn't doing it well enough – maybe I was disappointed with the script or storyline. But I'd still have to work at it for my own satisfaction. I couldn't come out with less than thinking that I'd tried for that. I'm never pleased.

The times I've been pleased in anything I've done, I could count on the fingers of one hand. And if you've been really good in something, it's harder next time because you've got that standard to live up to. What I loved about *Brookside* was that it was a continual testing and learning process. There had to be that element of fear, too, although, after a while, it did get a bit safe. When you lose that danger, it becomes less interesting to do. The last eighteen months, I found it less interesting – a bit samey – and that was a dilemma, really.

I had worked in a soap before, in *Coronation Street*. When it came along, I was so relieved to get some work. I had a baby and was quite poor. There was no ambition attached to it, it was purely practical. It was just about paying the bills, paying the mortgage, feeding the child – changing my career to a position where I earned better money. *Brookside* was the same. It was going to be regular and, what was exciting, it was new for me. Doing *Coronation Street* was also new for me because I'd never worked in television before. It was a challenge to learn something and from that I could sit back and assess whether it was right for me. It's like any situation I find myself in. I'll learn from it. *Brookside* certainly gave me a better standard of living. I played Sheila Grant for eight years. What was the life-saver for my character was that she was thrown into so many situations. I loved the mothering thing about her. I liked it best when she had the family around her and she loved her kids to death. Something went when the family drifted off. But that's real. That is what women have to deal with.

What was also good about Sheila was that older women don't get represented so often on television. Usually, it's younger women having passionate feelings or having the babies or being educated – which is why I suggested in the first place that she should get pregnant because they were always waiting for one of the younger couples to have a baby. I thought, 'Sheila's just got rid of her family with them all growing up. She's got interests. She's suddenly realized she's bright and she wants to expand her interests.' You see it all the time in women in their forties – 'I want to do this, that and the other, there's nothing to stop me' – and suddenly she's pregnant. Also, Sheila was a Catholic, so there was no way she could get rid of it. It was having to deal with the discipline of having a child at nearly fifty.

The part stretched me but it was a different sort of stretching – technical ability, really. I know now how to get a performance out quickly in front of a camera. We'd shoot three episodes in six days – rehearse one lot while we were shooting the next – like weekly rep, the same sort of head count. You get the lines under your belt, rehearse once, get that in front of the camera, then at the weekend learn more lines. But every so often, within that, you'd have a break.

The pressure would be on you for a few weeks, then it would drop back and you'd get rested.

What they try to do is 'major you', 'minor you', 'take you out', and you'd see that in *Coronation Street* or anything else. *EastEnders* takes people out, too, but they seem to use people a lot all the time. They tended not to do that with us, but then you'd get caught up in a storyline. One time it went on for six months. I wasn't in every episode but, if you're there, you're there. It was exhausting but, all the time, I was learning.

I'd love to make a film. We'd shoot on camera, not in the studio. It must be a joy just to shoot a couple of scenes a day. With us, they'd say, 'we're ready' and you'd go for it. We turned them over so quickly, it could be very frustrating. The good thing was they did get to know you and trust you and, if you had a good director, they'd say 'Are you happy with that, is there anything you want to change?'

In the main, directors didn't seem to stay with *Brookside* that long. They'd get a lot of good experience on camera – *Brookside* has got a certain reputation within the business. It's always been good-looking technically. So it attracted directors and they'd come for a year, eighteen months, then move on.

We had a dozen scriptwriters. Some were good and some had been there too long and lost that zing. (It's the same with actors, if they stay too long; they need someone to push them a bit.) My own favourite was Jimmy McGovern. I could do his scripts for ever. He writes beautifully for women. I think, if you're a good writer, you can write well, full stop. I often wondered how he *knew* I felt like that as a woman. It was absolutely right. Women writers often couldn't put that into your mouth; maybe they're too close. He topped for me any writer in that show and that was the difference for me, when he went, as it is for any actor: you're only as good as the tools you're given to work with. You get a good script and you take off, you don't have to sit rewriting or saying, 'My character wouldn't say that'. It can be very hard once you've started to rehearse, if you have to work on the script. I got very frustrated with that.

You do have an input but, if it's something to do with the character or the way a storyline is going, you've got to go with what they make you do. If that becomes unbearable, then the only step, really, is to leave. I hate to think of input as power because I think that's when you can't judge what you're doing. It's like people who want to have a say about the costumes they wear.

I think that's a danger, particularly in television soaps, because actors do like to be liked. Some people take on the character; it's not themselves, they're acting. The character has a certain way of dressing and a certain way of behaving. Now some other actors are almost the same as their character, there's no difference. I'm not saying there's anything wrong with it. That's what they want to be.

The danger is that, if you're playing yourself on the screen and you suddenly get a storyline where you're behaving rather nastily, you think, 'I can't do this, I've got to find a nice way round this because people will not like *me*'. Whereas I could be a crabby old cow and it was Sheila Grant that was the crabby old cow. It was nothing to do with me, so I could play the character to the hilt.

If you're playing yourself, it's very difficult if you're walking down the street and people are saying, she's a miserable bugger, or she's a nasty whatever, because they're making a statement about *you*. I saw actors get very upset about what they were being asked to do. Going into a pub, I was told, 'You're a ruddy this and you're a ruddy that', and I'd think, 'Well, it's only a character'. Those actors couldn't see the difference because they couldn't separate it from themselves.

I think it's all to do with the clothes. You want to be seen looking good, looking glamorous. There were times when I got into Sheila Grant's clothes and I felt so utterly depressed, but it was right for the character. It was a part although it was me playing her, so I put a lot of myself in. My friends never thought of me as Sheila because they know me so well. They would look at *Brookside* and see a totally different person. Physically, I didn't walk like her and, if you're playing somebody else, you do all sorts of things with your body like letting your body sag where you wouldn't normally.

The things Sheila stood for weren't me. I've no strong religious beliefs. When she was doing her anti-abortion run for the second time, I hated it in every fibre of my body. It was consistent with her character but not with mine. But I had to go for it because she went for it.

If I'd been playing me, how would I have been able to deal with people coming up to me in the street and saying, 'How dare you?' After her first anti-abortion run, I got letters saying, 'It's only a seed. How dare you, I'll never watch you again.' I used to think, 'Well, they can't separate either. It's their problem. It's not my problem because it is just a character.' I always made sure, when I was doing a newspaper interview, that they got that in: 'No, I don't believe in it. It's totally opposed to what I believe in.' I think most people knew that. But I did hate having to represent it.

In the beginning of *Brookside*, we all thrashed around together. Then the show got bigger and so did the whole organization. But you could still go to Phil Redmond, the producer, and say, 'Look, I need help, I don't like the way the character's going'. It was a small enough organization still to be able to go and iron things out and be told why the characters were behaving in a certain way because of where they were taking you.

I'm quite a fighter. I would stick to my guns and fight my corner, especially when I thought I was right. If the script wasn't good enough, I'd want to change it. I'm a bit of a perfectionist, as much as you can be in a soap, I suppose. But there is a particular danger in soaps. You have to ask yourself, 'Am I just frightened of making these lines work? Are they badly written, or is it an inability within me? Do I just want to make life easy for myself?' You've got to be very honest with yourself – try it, work with it before you say, 'Actually, this is crap, I can't make it work because people don't talk like that'.

I don't think it's as bad as it used to be coming out of a soap, but there's no knowing until you come out. It's very individual. Some of the people who've come out have done well but some people who you'd think would do well, didn't. I thought Anita Dobson would come out and just fly. She or her agent have not chosen right for her. I think she's really got an awful lot of talent and I expected her to go on a buzz and she didn't. So that's rather frightening for somebody like me coming out. It's like you just do not know what will happen to you and it might be that nobody will want to put you on the television because they associate you so strongly with one particular character.

What really changed things for me was when John McArdle (who played my husband, Billy Corkhill in *Brookside*) and I did a play at the Edinburgh Festival in 1989. On the first night, the audience went wild. It was a wonderful way to start the evening. Sometimes, though, it was a pain because you got a lot of people who were silly about it, women who just wanted to scream at John. I used to say, 'Your bloody fans are in again tonight.' It was a joke really but some nights it was a terrible battle just to play the scenes.

On the other hand, what was wonderful was that, 90 per

cent of the time, people came to see Billy and Sheila and, they would tell us in the bar afterwards, they'd have a shock when we came out that we weren't being those two, and then totally forgot about them and loved the play. Many of them had never been to the theatre before. That was so satisfying because that's what we set out to do. We didn't want to go out and just do a Billy and Sheila *Brookside* show. We set out to do a play because we were two actors working together feeling frustrated and needing a new challenge.

We'd continually been asked to do theatre work during the period I'd been at *Brookside* and never been able to do it. Then the chance came up at Bolton, which was near enough to do a two-hander. John said, 'What about us doing *Decadence* by Steven Berkoff?' and I thought, 'great'. Then I thought, 'Oh no, we can't do *Decadence*. Imagine all the old ladies in Bolton zooming off to see John and me as Billy and Sheila fornicating around the stage.' A bit too much to bear. Anyway, we took that on board first, and that it was Bolton. Then we went to *Brookside*, to get their OK. Then Jim Cartwright became resident playwright at Bolton and it all just happened. Edinburgh Festival picked up on it and offered us a space. And now we're going to bring it to London. It couldn't have worked out more perfectly, but we took a risk doing it. I think that's why people stay in soaps. The risks coming out are so great.

What I'd really like to do is film. And I'd love to go to the National or RSC. I really need to test myself with those big companies. I've done Restoration before, played *The Country Wife* and loved it. I'd like to do the big Shakespeares, like Sheila Hancock has done at the RSC.

It is difficult when you've got children. You have to consider them, but there comes a point where you think, if you're unhappy, you're not going to do the kid much good either. I think there's only so much you can sacrifice in your life. I would never sacrifice my son's happiness. Maybe I'm a bit selfish but I don't want to sacrifice myself either. Having said that, you still just can't take off and do whatever you want to do. You always have to make compromises. It's a bloody struggle because you cannot, as a mother, be that selfish. How do I then find a happy medium where I can be fulfilled and he isn't suffering because of my needs?

I always wanted to be an actor. If I was as wealthy as hell, or had an extremely wealthy husband, I would still want to work. So I know I'm not working because I have to. But I also *am* working because I have to. It's extremely hard to balance it all. I have no choice. I've got to earn a living. I haven't got a man behind me. I haven't got any other finance behind me except what I bring through the door. So I have to work.

At the moment, I can work in the field I love. I've spent twenty odd years working and, 90 per cent of that time, it's been in the theatre and it's been acting. I've been extremely lucky, although it's not always been well paid.

'The bug' started at school when I played The Witch in *The Tinderbox*. I thought, 'I like it here, I feel right on this stage.' That was where I belonged. I could function. I mean, I am a *mess* of insecurity, of vulnerability, inferiority complex, all those things. But on stage, I'm not a mess any more.

Of course, there's the 'I'm not doing it right, I can't do this' kind of feelings but, in the main, I'm in control. I feel good and, because I've now been doing it for so long, I know where my limitations are. I can be vulnerable and criticized along the way and that's OK. What I also like about it is that you're continually learning. Your life is never still. I've always loved change, the excitement of moving on. I hate anything that's the same, hate knowing today what's going to happen tomorrow. Love the acting lifestyle. So it's all packaged up for my personality. In a slot. That's what I'm meant to be, an actor.

I'm extremely lucky, I know. But when you're growing up in Huyton in Liverpool and you go to the local careers office and say, 'I want to be an actor', and your parents are working class and there are no actors in the family – they all think you're insane! There's nobody to help you, no one to advise you. All I had was this very strong knowledge inside me: that's what I want to do.

I was an only child but my mother came from a huge family of twelve who are all still alive. My father's family was quite huge and extended, too. So there was a very close, clan-like family thing. That can be a bit swamping some-times, a bit stifling.

I went to the Webber Douglas drama school. It was bliss because it was out of my experience. I remember it so clearly and I loved every minute of it. I loved being in London, I loved being away from home – not that I wasn't a happy child. I was a very happy, secure child, but I just loved being away. I think it's something about being an individual, living in a flat, and just being on my own in London. I just *grew*. And to be doing things about the theatre and acting, it was extraordinary.

I was frightened to death at first. I also had a very strong Liverpool accent and made friends fast with a girl from Birkenhead, Val, and a boy, Mike, from Birmingham, because all three of us were very working class with strong accents. Everybody else seemed to be from very middle- or upper-class backgrounds. There were all these beautiful women with long, blonde, flowing tresses, looking like models and speaking with plummy accents. I used to think, 'What am I doing here?' We three didn't speak to anybody except each other because we thought we'd be found out.

All that went into reverse shortly after I got there. My

timing was perfect! Ralph Jago, who hadn't been there in our first term, took over and totally changed what we were doing. I loved him, I learnt so much from him. One day he said, 'Who's working class in this group?' We three raised our arms – reluctantly, like, 'We're found out, the shame is upon us'. And he said, 'This is the new fire of the theatre. This is the changing world of theatre.' We just *preened*: 'Anybody want to talk to us, like?' It was wonderful. It helped our confidence so much although we still had to struggle with getting rid of our accents. It's no use going to audition at the RSC with a thick accent.

They used to say, and it would baffle me, 'Now, we want you to lose your accent but keep the colour of it'. I used to think, 'What! I ca-an't do that'. 'I ca-annot do that.' I knew what they meant but I didn't know how to achieve it. The only way you could do it was to go totally the other way and go very posh.

I shared a dressing room once with Glenda Jackson for a charity up in Liverpool, and I kept thinking, 'This is a real actress'. I still have those feelings within me, that I don't think I'm a real actress. I keep thinking I'll get found out. Judi Dench and Maureen Lipman, Glenda and Peggy Ashcroft, they're the grand people. They've done the RSC and the National. They're real actresses and I feel choked in their company. I feel what I felt when I went to drama school, which is a terrible inferiority complex about discovering that I'm nothing because I always feel as if I'm starting off again and have to prove myself.

I think, probably I would tend to freeze at the National in case I got found out – 'What on earth is she doing here? Get back to the tax office' – never really feeling that I was included. I think a lot of actors probably feel the same. We're a terribly insecure breed of people.

* * *

I spent eleven, twelve years with Coventry Theatre-In-Education. It was an extraordinary experience, and terribly different theatre in that you had control over your material, control over the content, and there actually was a political level.

Working with children, I learnt an awful lot about education and how you create plays for children of different ages and different needs. I found I liked doing the research, working in a team and spinning off ideas. You'd find a subject, go away and research it and have to come back, write scenes and do improvisations – create a play really. You were being tested all the time. Once you'd put it together, you then had to go along and do it for kids and see if you'd got it right. I found that – the whole gamut from A to Z – an amazing creative process.

It was the politics as well. Coming from a working-class background, my parents had always been politically aware. They always voted. That generation did, they knew the value of it. I remember as a kid seeing them go off, all dressed up to place their vote, it was that important. It had been a hard-won fight to get the vote. They recognized that.

I was always aware of the world in which I lived because it hadn't been easy. As a student too, I'd been in Grosvenor Square, I was on the anti-Vietnam march. That had a big influence on my life. Then the Industrial Relations Act and all that business had started me really becoming very aware of world politics, and politics in this country, and I started making assessments about it.

I'd worked in Theatre-in-Education at the Cockpit Theatre in London for three years but it was political with a small 'p'. Also, we did set texts. When the Coventry team came up to do a lecture demonstration, I suddenly realized they were talking about the real world in which we all live. It was socially aware politics and it was being able to bring that to kids and make them aware of the real world that so impressed me, not feeding them second-rate stuff. I was gobsmacked and I thought, 'I want to be with this team'. They were also incredibly articulate.

The work certainly had an effect on me. Because I was putting myself in a position of making children question, I had to question myself. I apply that as much to my work now as I did in Coventry. You have to examine your own motives, examine the world about you, stay open to experiences and not judge. That's why I get so upset about bigotry. People say, 'I'd never behave like that', but, if you've never been tested or challenged, how do you know?

I try to be as truthful as I can in my work. It's easier to be truthful on camera, you can't run away from it. It goes right into the eyes. In theatre, you've got to project more. That's why it evaporates sometimes. One of the few things I would still put down as feeling proud of was playing Charlotte Corday in *Marat Sade* at drama school. Glenda Jackson had just done it. I hadn't seen it and I was really glad that I hadn't. For the first time, I lost myself in a part. I'm not surprised because it was a very political play.

I always feel as if I don't really know an awful lot about feminism. Anybody could come and catch me out about it and they often do. But I really believe I am equal with men – in fact, a hell of a lot more equal than a lot of men. I believe in equality. It's instinctive. I campaign the same as I would fight for blacks or gays or whatever because for me it's about equal rights. I hate things from men like 'keep your woman down'. Yet I know I can slot right back into being the little woman: 'Oh, I've got to look nice' and all that. I'm learning though. I look nice for me now – except when sex comes along, then I'm all over the place.

*   *   *

I love nothing more than acting. I'd miss it if I wasn't doing it. I couldn't ever see a day when I wouldn't want to do it. If I didn't have any work, I've got a lovely idea for a one-woman TIE show. The pleasure, I suppose is to do with communication. That creates an adrenalin of its own. Yet, you don't get that when you're doing television, when you can't see the audience. So it's not *just* about that. It's still about testing yourself and living out fantasies. It's like playing games, a child playing games.

JUDI DENCH

'That won't do at all, Miss Dench'

pic credit: Sophie Vauner

Born York. Trained Central School of Speech and Drama.

Regarded as one of Britain's finest actresses, Judi Dench has been described by critic Michael Coveney as the heiress apparent to Edith Evans, Sarah Siddons and Ellen Terry 'who has brought tragedy into the world of fitted cupboards'. She is indeed an actress of contrasts, capable of turning laughter to tears and vice versa in a moment – not for nothing is she known in the business as a legendary 'corpser' with a humour just this side of respectable anarchy.

The husky voice – with the heart-tweaking catch in it – has been used as effectively to encompass Chekhov's Madame Ranyevskaya, and the lovably bossy Laura of *A Fine Romance*, as it has *Cabaret*'s Sally Bowles while Juliet, Beatrice, Viola, Portia, Lady Bracknell, Mother Courage, Juno, Cleopatra, and an especially sexually ravaged Lady Macbeth (opposite Ian McKellen), are all other leading roles that she has stamped with her authority. Yet she has, too, the distinctive gift of merging so inside a role as to become almost unrecognizable – as Barbara, the mousey wife of *Pack of Lies*, discovering her next door neighbours to be Russian spies in London suburbia, awaking from sleeping sickness in Pinter's *A Kind of Alaska*, or as the mother of a thalidomide-damaged son in the television play *On Giant's Shoulders*.

Films include Peter Hall's *Four in the Morning*, Titania in his *A Midsummer Night's Dream*, *84 Charing Cross Road*, Kenneth Branagh's *Henry V* and scene-stealing gems in *A Handful of Dust*, the Merchant/Ivory *A Room with A View* (with Maggie Smith), and *Wetherby*.

Recipient of over twenty drama awards for Best Actress, she received the OBE in 1970, and the DBE in 1988.

She is married to actor Michael Williams and lives in London and on the Surrey/Sussex border. They have one daughter, Finty.

When I was younger, I only ever wanted to be a dancer or a designer. My mother and father were both very keen on the theatre and, as children, we were all taken to see pantomimes and things like *Peter Pan*, Gilbert and Sullivan and so on. I remember seeing *Cuckoo in the Nest* and being completely hysterical about it, I laughed so much.

My father, who was a doctor, was born in Dorset but lived in Ireland all his life. My mother was from Dublin and so they were both brought up in Dublin. His practice then took him to Tildsley in Manchester, where my brothers were born, and then to York, where I was born.

After school, I had a year off and went to York Art School where I did a course on theatre design. Then I went to Stratford and saw a production of *King Lear* with Michael Redgrave and Marius Goring. It had an amazing set which, overnight, changed my mind. I suddenly thought, '*That* is the most *supreme* design and that is the kind of designer I would want to be – but my imagination would always let me down.'

So I decided to go to drama school and went to the Central School of Speech and Drama where Jeff, my brother, had been. I was really rather half-hearted about everything. I just didn't know what I wanted to do. However, at the end of our first year, Walter Hudd, who was Head of Production, gave me a lot of encouragement about a mime I did which I'd completely forgotten about and did absolutely off the cuff. I thought, 'Well, perhaps there's something here that I really must concentrate on.'

I had three years at Central and loved it. Vanessa Redgrave was in the same year. So was Julian Belfrage who was to become my agent. In my final year, they were looking for somebody at the Old Vic to play Ophelia and I was sent along. I thought it was just a walk-on but Michael Benthall actually cast me as Ophelia.

I think I have been incredibly lucky with my career. It has just rolled on – extraordinary really, a charmed life. A lot of my good luck, I think, is to do with being in the right place at the right time. I mean, to go to the Old Vic as your first job as Ophelia! It just happened that they were at the end of the five-year plan, and the only play they repeated was *Hamlet*, the first year with Richard Burton, then the last year with John Neville. Michael Benthall just happened to be looking for somebody when I just happened to be coming out of drama school. That is coincidence and luck.

Of course, ghastly things have happened, like my Achilles tendon snapping in two when I was rehearsing for *Cats*. I don't say it was meant to happen, but when I did the Pinter play, *A Kind of Alaska*, at the National, on the first night when I had to walk across the floor to Paul Rogers, I remember thinking, 'I wouldn't have had any experience of having to walk as an adult for the first time' – she'd had sleeping sickness for twenty-eight years – 'if I hadn't had that accident'. I remember thinking 'maybe there is a pattern to things' because, when I was recovering, I had absolutely to start from scratch and remember how to put the heel down and what to do with the ball of the foot. So you never know. I'm waiting for something to come up next year where being laid up for eight weeks with a broken ankle, as I am now, might come in handy!

I stayed with the Vic for four seasons, playing Ophelia, walking on and understudying everyone. Juliet in Zeffer-elli's *Romeo and Juliet* seems to be the one most people remember. The critics thought I was absolutely frightful except for Ken Tynan and Milton Shulman. Then, on the last night, there was all this standing up and shouting and cheering.

I think one of the reasons it was remembered was because John Stride and I did actually look like children. Down the

176

ages, the two parts had always been played by quite established actors. Suddenly, it became a very lively play and a tragedy about two very young people who were totally bewildered and knew only the passion of love, not two rather romantic people who, if not quite settled, were quite able to conduct themselves and know what was happening.

I don't think that early good luck was to do with looks. I mean, I'm not tall and leggy. In fact, Michael Benthall kept saying, 'How tall are you? I suppose we could put you in heels', and I kept thinking, 'Why is this so important to him?' There was a lot of concern of this kind because you had to have a 'matching pair'. I never really understood, until I came to direct myself and had to match Benedict and Beatrice, how vital 'matching' is. The pair don't have to be compatible although, of course, it's wonderful if they are, and it doesn't matter about colour. It's something to do with physical compatability so that you can really believe that those two people really have got this tremendous bond between them. It's all right in a comedy if you haven't got a match but it simply won't do if it's a romantic or lyrical play.

Peter Hall says in his book on directing *Antony and Cleopatra* that he looked for a long time for a matching pair. Finally he put Anthony Hopkins and myself together. We're both rather stockily built and the pair matched very well.

Opposites can work perfectly too, that can be wonderful. It's a bit like having the luxury of being able to choose to do *the* most different thing to the last thing you did – a part that I *know* the general feeling is I'm quite unsuitable for. I love that. With Cleopatra, people used to throw their eyes up and go, 'Oh my god'. They used to almost laugh in my face. That's right, of course. You don't think of Cleopatra as my kind of person, you think of her as this extraordinary Egyptian woman who should be clever, sinuous, probably tall and all that.

The same kind of thing applied with Lady Macbeth. I first played the part with John Neville in Africa in 1963 before I played it again for Trevor Nunn in 1976. Later, with Lady Bracknell, I was totally unsuitable for that, as well!

When I came to do *Cabaret*, I'd never done any singing before, except once in *The Double Dealer* at the Old Vic when Michael Benthall said, 'We can't have that, it won't do at all, Miss Dench'. It was only two lines! I had to speak them in the end.

What I like is doing as many different things as possible in the theatre at the same time. I like being in a repertoire of four or five plays. My happiest days were at the National Theatre doing *The Importance of Being Ernest* and *A Kind of Alaska*, and then, in 1987, *Antony* and *Entertaining Strangers*. And all those plays at the Old Vic, I never had a night off. You're kept very much on your toes because you haven't got the luxury of having run it the night before. It's like a permanent first night and that keeps it very alive; doing a play eight times a week is a killer. Frankie Howerd once said we're the only profession who every single night at exactly the same time have to pretend we're doing something for the first time in our lives. That's why I like knowing friends are there because that's a help. You can tell the story specifically to somebody, not a mass of people that you can't see.

I've got the advantage of looking younger than fifty-six. Long may it continue! I expect finding parts will get harder as time goes on. There are still not enough parts written for women although there are some really remarkable women playwrights now and I think that the whole question of women is much more seriously looked at. But it will always be unsatisfying, I'm afraid. The profession's over-crowded anyway, the men have a hard time but the women have a worse time. I'm going to put my trust in the wheelchair parts myself. I'm going to play all these juveniles in some kind of chair.

I would like to have played Hilda Wengel in *The Master Builder*. And I would like to have played Cressida at some point – I remember seeing Dottie Tutin being simply wonderful in Peter Hall's production, and Helen Mirren with Michael [Williams]. I would like to have played Rosalind although I don't like the play very much. The difficulty there, is to get a Celia smaller than me, because Rosalind has to say, 'Because I'm somewhat taller, I'll call myself Ganymede'. So that's a pity.

The number of good women's parts in the classical repertoire is actually quite limited. After a certain age, there's the Duchess in *All's Well*, Volumnia in *Coriolanus*, one of the mad queens in *Richard III* and Lady Britomart in *Major Barbara*. I suppose I could get up in drag in *Saint Joan* and play the Bishop of Beauvais. I've never wanted to play Hamlet though. Good gracious no; so tiring, all those lines.

I can't say I've really felt any particular disadvantage as a woman. Egos in rehearsal can all be difficult. That's just rehearsal behaviour. You get some actors who behave really well, and some who don't. It's nothing to do with men and women, it's to do with personalities. Sometimes they're very unsure, like we all are, and some people have amazing ways of recovery and some people don't. Some people are able to sublimate their anxiety and take it home with them and work it out somehow there, and some people can't. Some people need the rehearsal room floor. I've never found that to do with male or female. I've just found it to do with the actual persona of the individual.

I'm awful at making my own choices. All the choices I've made have been terrible. I wait for somebody else to suggest a part I should play. Peter Hall said, 'I've found a great part for you. You've got to play Cleopatra, but we've got to find a fella.' It was Peter who also suggested Lady Bracknell and it was Frank Dunlop and Trevor Nunn who suggested Lady Macbeth.

I'm not good with my own choice because I don't think you see yourself in the right terms. I don't see myself as anything, any more. I just see this person with a great big green baize bag which I drag around full of bits of performances and faces and things that I can take out of it, who's available for panto or whatever. I take out a face and put it on and say 'No, this is not what's needed' and put it back in again.

It's nothing special, it's what every actor has, because everybody who's an actor has to have a bank and they have to have a freezer – perhaps not a freezer, that's too cold a thing – but they have to have some kind of memory bank, a larder so that they know they have something to draw on. That's what pleased me most about playing Juno. A couple of critics said, 'It's somebody we'd never seen before, with a voice and a walk and everything.' Those are the things that please me, not necessarily the part. I did feel very, very immersed in Juno. I love that kind of commitment to a play and the feeling that it had used up such a lot of me. Actually, on the first performance of *Antony and Cleopatra*, there was so much for me to be concerned and taken up by – not least, being thrown off the thirteen-foot monument at the end – that there was only room to tell the story. There was no room to think, 'Oh, my god, this is the first night'.

I don't want, if possible, to have a label but I know that people need to label you. I wish it wasn't like that because that's how you create a kind of magic – when people imagine that what's going to come out of a hat is a white rabbit and what comes out from your left sleeve is a string of mackerel! Those are the balls I like to keep in the air. That's the kind of surprise I like to create.

Funnily enough, I'm no good at a party. I'm not good at small-talk and I can't make any kind of speech at all. They say, 'Of course, you can do that if you're an actress.' No, of course, you can't necessarily do that if you're an actress. Maybe there is a kind of escape thing there, maybe it is the luxury of being able to be a lot of other people.

I've enjoyed every part I've played except, perhaps, for Portia. I loathed her. I don't think anything good comes out of the end of *The Merchant of Venice*. I wouldn't mind if Shylock came out of it well, but he doesn't. The Christians are a frightful bunch, too. Then Portia chooses at the end to play a rather nasty and unpleasant joke on her husband which rightly should misfire and he should divorce her and then it would be a wonderful play. I don't mind playing unsympathetic characters at all. I longed, for example, to play Regan. I don't particularly want sympathy for my character unless that's the intention of the author. I think it's good to try and make things work, but you can't just come on being a villain from the beginning. People are not like that. We're all so multi-layered that it's only worth trying to find those layers so that you *see* this person – and I don't mean to excuse them in any kind of way. What I like to show is the *reason* for this person being the way they are – 'this is the formula for this person'.

I tried with Regan, but it's very difficult with those three girls at the beginning of *Lear* because you get the two ugly sisters and you get Cinderella. From the beginning, Regan and Goneril are saying spiteful things. I think Lear behaves very unnecessarily, too, but I also think you should understand *why* those girls are like that. Unfortunately you know they're going to get their comeuppance from the beginning and that's a pity.

I remember during *Macbeth*, I said to Trevor Nunn,

'There ought to be children who come to this who maybe think that they *don't* do the murder.' There should be that question mark. I think Lady Macbeth is what she is because she's *obsessed* by her husband. What he wants, she is determined to get for him. If he wants her to kill her cousin, she says, 'Right, we'll kill him. If that's what you want, that's what you'll get. If that's what stands in the way of your ambition, I'll do it.' That's not painting her any whiter but at least it's giving a relationship between them of passion, certainly on her part, and tremendous ambition and greed. But if you present her as this wicked queen from the start, then why does she invoke the spirits to take away her femininity and say to them, 'Please, see me through. I want to do this. Let me forget the weaker side of me so that I can carry out this murder against my own cousin.' Then you see the breaking down of a real person because she loses everything including the one thing that she prizes above all, which is her relationship with her husband. Then, to me, it seems to make sense.

Sometimes, I have found it hard to find the reality in these women. I just couldn't find any in Gertrude. She seems to have a very unchartered course, although Coral Browne, when she played it at the Vic, was supreme, really tragic and bewildered. I used to watch her and think, 'This is a wonderful part'. Well, it's not a wonderful part. Coral Browne is a wonderful actress. But I couldn't find it. It's beaten me, I'm afraid, as Regan has. My Regan was just very funny, hysterically funny.

I do love doing comedy. It's so rewarding to hear a great gale of laughter because then you know you've hit the button right on the head. Very gratifying. And I love to work with people who are great comic actors. When Michael did his farce performance, *Two Into One*, my mouth dropped open. He has *brilliant* timing. Donald Sinden is wonderful, too, although he does go over the top sometimes, especially during *your* bits. But my admiration is really unbounded for both of them.

It's the whole business, the company, that I enjoy, it's not really the part, ever. It's the company and the set up and the rehearsal period and the *jokes*. Probably most of all – the jokes.

It's also to do with communication and the fact that you can manipulate an audience. It's a kind of magic that you can, on the good days, get them to laugh, to cry, to feel anger, to feel pity . . . and that makes you feel you've achieved something. That's what you're all about.

Elizabeth Spriggs really serves up the play. So do a lot of actors but I just remember watching Lizzie, as well as giving the most extraordinary performance in *Major Barbara* and *Women Beware Women*, really serve the play up. That's really what it's about; telling the story, the author's story, to that audience. It's not to do with one's ego, it's to do with the collective ego of everybody and somehow going through that, in order to *present* a perfect ball that you can then bat across the net.

Kenneth Branagh is very keen on having an ensemble, where you have a basic company of, say, thirty people and in it you have young people who gradually will grow up through that company to play the leads (like Roger Rees did at Stratford and as everybody did at the Vic). That's marvellous because so much of learning our craft is watching other people. I never went to the dressing room during *Hamlet* at the Vic. I stood all the time watching the show. I still do it. When I'm directing, I always say you must not just watch during rehearsal, but also during the performance itself. You have to be very finely attuned with that all-seeing eye and the all-hearing ear. That's why it's always a good thing to get down early for your call so that you can hear the pace of the scene, hear the audience reaction to it in case you have to pick up on the pace if something's gone much slower or something's gone too fast and you suddenly have to pull it back. It's like permanently riding a difficult horse.

Working in television's very different. It's a lovely job. And of course, as somebody said to us when we were doing *A Fine Romance*, to reach the same audience you get for one episode, you would have to play fourteen years at the Aldwych *every night*. But reactions to you change entirely. Suddenly you get people saying, 'Is this your first job?'. *A Fine Romance* is all that people talk to me about now, they never talk about Lady Macbeth!

The script for *A Fine Romance* was actually sent to us while Michael was away in Greece filming, and I read it and thought it was very funny. I always object to situation comedies where everyone is always dressed up to the nines, and look as though they've stepped straight out of *Elle* magazine. I thought these people are much more like life.

Mike tried to get through to me for days and couldn't. When he finally did ring, I said, 'Look, we've been sent this series'. He said, 'Does it make you laugh?' I said, 'Yes'. He said, 'Accept it.' I did accept it on his behalf and that was a really fearfully difficult thing to do.

Funnily enough, when we'd done it and the next series came up, I was away in Bangkok. When I phoned home and Mike said, 'The next series has come', I said, 'Would it make me laugh? If yes, accept it.'

I'd never do that again because the responsibility is so great. I mean, I think I know Michael's sense of humour, but it may be that he wouldn't have laughed so much. Not everything that makes him laugh makes me laugh, otherwise one would be so much the same person. So it was quite a risk, but in the end, it was OK, it was all right.

Television, though, doesn't have the same kind of feeling about it as you get in the theatre. It's a one-off thing and also you get that awful feeling the next day of knowing *exactly* how you should have played the scene. Then it's too late! Even more so with filming. Sometimes in television you can re-do a scene. We re-shot a couple of scenes on the last television we did, *Can you hear me thinking*, where Michael and I play the parents of a boy with schizophrenia. There were certain scenes that we just suddenly thought had gone awry. In the theatre, you have got the chance to get it better, to get nearer the goal each time.

When our daughter, Finty, was a baby, I didn't particularly want to be doing television, I didn't want to miss out on the days when she was a tiny baby. When she started school, it was much more convenient to be on television than in the theatre because then I could be off in the evening when she was home. After she was born, I remember thinking that I'd never experienced *real* sorrow before I had her. Everything made me cry – the experience of many women, I think. One day, Michael was out and when he came back, I was watching a programme about wild dogs and I was *completely* hysterical. Just because this young dog had been turned out of the pack, had her puppies and then kept foraging and the pack kept coming in and killing the puppies. Well, I was fit to be tied. Somehow you feel as though your sorrow has never been plumbed to its lowest depth and it was as if it did release a trap door. Somehow something dropped further. I don't know whether that connects with my acting at all; perhaps it does, somewhere.

I don't mind whether I'm doing classical or new plays although I don't often read scripts. Michael usually reads them and tells me. I read very, very little indeed. Now that I've decided to direct, I'll have to read more. Everybody has different ways of remembering lines. You have to, because if you can't do *that*, you can't start. It's like typing. You can't be a typist if you can't type. Shakespeare's easy because you can hear the metre of it. If you dry, you just say the number of syllables. What is difficult is playing things like Shaw and Wilde because they're perfectly phrased and we don't speak correct English any more. We put things round the wrong way. That's got a kind of wonderful metre about it, too. And all those eighteenth-century plays. I played Millament in *The Way of the World* – with difficulty.

Every single play throws up a different problem. It's all difficult really, but the pleasures are immense. It's rewarding, exciting, it's putting yourself on the line, it's going through a hoop, it's a way of making a living, it's frightening, very frightening. And yes, I do get stage fright, I'd be much more frightened if I didn't get it. So it's a tremendous mixture of things but it's mostly people. It's the audience, I suppose, you ultimately do it for, but it's also the interplay between actor/director, actor/actress, all of us together.

When I was young, there was more of a stricture on theatre in that you called everyone Mr or Miss – Mr Gwyilm, Miss Browne – and you didn't suddenly say 'Wouldn't it be better in this scene . . .' But now, of course, thanks very much to the RSC – I hate the word 'house style', but that was the way – there's a much more democratic way of going about things and you can suggest things and say 'What do you think, if we did such and such?' It's like a kind of melting pot in which everybody – director and actors – make a contribution, which is what I learned from all my years at the RSC with Peter Hall, Trevor Nunn, John Barton and Terry Hands, and which I then applied, when I came to direct. I said, 'I don't have a concept for this, I know what I want it to look like, I know the period of time I want it to take place in but I don't have a concept and I want that to be something that we all find the level of together.' And I think that's the best way of working.

I didn't ask to direct, Ken Branagh asked me. I thought he

was going to ask me to play a part, but he didn't. Instead, he asked me to direct *Much Ado*. It took me quite a long time to decide. Directing feels very different. I find the actual process more tiring and not nearly so satisfying as being in the play and trying to make it work. When it comes to opening, you know the play is going to be taken away from you – the baby's adopted by the audience. The cast don't want you any more. You see things going wrong and you can't really do much about it. It's rather like being a parent.

I've been asked to do a lot more directing, but I don't know whether I can unless I get stronger and more bossy. It doesn't come naturally to me. A lot of good directors have never been actors. I think it's probably easier for an actor who's having a problem to be directed by another actor, because they might be able to see the way through the problem and show them a kind of guideline. But if you stuck to just that, you'd negate a lot of very good directors. Peter Hall was never an actor – well, he was an amateur actor at university – but he knows absolutely how to tell you, how to help you chart your way through a play. And Frank Hauser, who directed me in many plays at the Oxford Playhouse, was never an actor. Being a good director is really about having a very particular eye and being very watchful.

I was very keen on verse speaking when I came to direct *Much Ado*, and I was able to pass on those things that Peter Hall and Trevor Nunn and John Barton had taught me. I hope in time they will be passed on to somebody else. Of course, each generation adapts as times change, but verse speaking just gets worse. It's something that should be learned and passed on. There's no substitute for that.

I don't feel competitive although I have felt envious of other people's talent even though I am a Dame. I don't quite know what it's for, though. I never asked. I didn't go and say, 'Please what is this for?' I get sent up terribly. Dame

Judith they call me, not Judi. When Maggie Smith became a Dame I said, 'You won't be Maggie any more – it'll be Dame Margaret now.' No messing about, proper names only if you're a Dame. 'Dear Dame Dench', I have a lot of the time. I think to myself, would you say 'Dear Sir Gielgud'?

There are still things left to do. I'd like to achieve the kind of notices I got for Juno about something else. I *long* for that again – that thing of absolutely not being recognized. My strength, though, is that I'm quite good in a company. I'm a company person and that's a kind of strength to me too – I need that, selfishly, for myself as well. It's probably why I have never done a one-woman show. I don't know who I'd get ready for. I don't know who I'd sit in the dressing room with or have jokes with.

If you're going to work as a company, it must be a unit, it mustn't be a lot of people pushing against each other. I do feel I've got to look after other people a little – no, not quite perhaps look after them, that's not quite the right word. I like everyone to feel part of it all. We're a unit, and we're a unit in that we should be responsible for each other. It sounds rather cosy, and I don't mean it to be cosy – I just mean it to be a company.

CARMEN MUNROE

'My life has become bigger'

Born British Guyana.

One of the elder stateswomen of British black actresses, Carmen Munroe appears regularly on Channel 4's popular black soap, *Desmond's*, but also scored a great personal success as Sister Margaret Alexander, the over-zealous pastor of a Harlem 'store-front' church in James Baldwin's *The Amen Corner* and, before that, as the mother in Lorraine Hansbury's *A Raisin in the Sun* (both presented by the small north London Tricycle Theatre).

She made her debut in Tennessee Williams's *Period of Adjustment* at the Royal Court in 1962 but a turning point, in Munroe's view, was when she was cast as Orinthia, the King's mistress in Shaw's *The Apple Cart* at the Mermaid in 1970, (with John Neville as King Magnus) – the first time, she says, that she had been cast in a major role that had not been written for a black actress.

She has also played a leading role in the development of Black Theatre in this country, appearing in plays by writers such as Caryl Phillips (*Strange Fruit*) and Edgar White (*Redemption Song*). She directed James Saunders's *Alas, Poor Fred*, and also the British premiere of *Remembrance* by Caribbean poet and writer, Derek Walcott in the 1987 Black Theatre Season at London's Art Theatre.

She has made numerous bread and butter appearances in such television series as *Playschool*, *General Hospital* and *Crown Court*.

She lives in London.

I was born in Guyana (then British Guyana) and came to Britain in the early fifties, when I was in my teens.

For years, people at home wanted to go to America. When people who had gone there came back, we thought they looked so *well*, so glamorous, as if they were all living in Hollywood. But if you come to England, it's a serious experience. It isn't about looking well. It's just about being serious. We were all serious in my time, and perhaps too sheltered. In Guyana, you don't leave home until you get married and live in your own house. There is no such thing as living in an apartment away from home, however big the family is. In some cases, married couples even live with one or other set of in-laws because they haven't found a house yet, and they are still bound by the laws of the house – and I do mean the *laws* of the house: 'this done this way' and 'that done at that time'. It was the kind of discipline that existed in Dickensian times. I think it was good.

We were a large family, all living in a large house. Altogether, there were nine brothers and sisters. Then there was my father's mother and an aunt who would be there, or another aunt who lived across the road. And cousins coming to stay. It was open house generally – and not only the family. My mother is still in touch with people who helped us in the house over the years. Now they've become part of the family.

We were certainly middle class, if you had to put a name to it. The family was comfortable, if not well off. You didn't have to be well off at home to have people helping you. If I had remained at home, I would have worked in the civil service. There would have been no problem in finding a job. I came to England, though, to study. I did Ophthalmic Optics for a year.

As a child, one of my dreams had been to dance, to be a ballerina or an ice-skater. Anything that had a look of freedom and flying and moving through the air appealed to me then and still does. I hadn't seen much classical dance at home except in films. If you had said that you wanted to be a dancer at home, a lot of people would have said, 'What do you mean dancer? Everybody's a dancer. Dance if you want to. Dance for the joy of it.' So to ask to be a dancer, to go to be trained, was a little out of the ordinary in those days. I did do some dance when I came to England. I danced with a West Indian troupe, who were a sort of mixture of Creole, African and Martha Graham.

In my early days, I was dancing as well as working in an office. That was my 'straight' job. I also became quite involved with the Movement for Colonial Freedom, one of the organizations in England in the late fifties that was trying to allay racial prejudice and promote a more intelligent understanding of the members of the Commonwealth. I'd be asked by them to perform – read poetry, dance or compere programmes. I also remember working with a group at the West Indian Students Union where I'd go after work. There was a drama group, too. We used to do productions, exercises and classes. To me, this was a means of expressing a kind of energy and awareness of self, being able to reach a lot of people without actually having to talk to them individually.

I had a strong sense of how much we are taught to *deny* self. A lot of the time, I lived inside myself. I think society expected you to do that. Self-awareness is earned. Back in Guyana, there's a lot of living outside *physically*, but not *internally*. I can go out on the street there and have a wonderful time at Carnival with people jumping up and down – but there's a *person* living inside that person that is all screwed up and tight and not really *being*. For me it was like that. I felt 'framed', internally oppressed.

I don't think it's unique. What I'm trying to describe is a psychological condition that is probably quite common but for me was very choking, very restricting. Being on stage was one way of going inside in a public way. Speaking words became a natural extension of the dance.

I've always loved words as a means of expression. I went to a high school with a headmaster who was an exponent of the English language. It was beautiful to listen to him speak. There wasn't one word you could use in place of the ones that he used. He was a master of his language. The schoolmaster in Derek Walcott's play *Remembrance*, which I directed in the Black Theatre Season a few years ago, was like that. Walcott is a brilliant man. He loves words, too. That's why I did the play. I just loved it for the way he uses language. I thought, 'This is not going to make me a brilliant director, I probably won't be able to direct.' I just wanted to *soak* up the whole feeling of the thing.

English English was the language we were expected to speak and take exams in at school. I can't write patois, I only know how it is spoken. There is a movement now to put it down on paper and make it a recognized language. But it's difficult to read. I can only hear it and feel it. Our English came straight out of the book. It's quite funny, I have to laugh.

This is a generalization, but the thing about cultural influence, in this case British colonial influence, is that you can't not want it, it's there, you're brought up with it. The question is how to make it a positive force in your life – discarding the negative and striving to find roots. That sense of your own identity has to evolve out of an accumulation of past experience. It has to do that, otherwise it's not real; it's an empty thing. It goes in phases. There is the first experience; and then a mixture of that experience and what one is experiencing now. Then, after that comes finding out what was useful in the past, what's useful in the present and how it can be used now in the creation of our own black theatre.

I don't think I've changed drastically except in so far as change is inevitable. What I've grown to understand is that the individual must create a life for himself or herself. I must have my own focus and what I mustn't do is to *frame* myself. There's this picture and that's it, framed – nowhere to go, nothing more can happen, when what I really feel is that I must allow things to happen all the time and live in such a way that I can absorb and express all the times that I've lived in. It's not easy. I don't have that freedom. I don't write the stuff that I work in, I don't employ myself. I work within certain constraints, but, because of my Buddhist practice, I've been able to create a freedom within those constraints.

It was quite hard establishing myself as an actor for some years, and not just as an actor but as a member of this English society – because of my West Indian background – as it was for West Indians generally. There was a particularly heady time between 1965 and 1975 when I was fortunate enough to work with directors who had an adventurous approach to their work. I was very successfully cast, for example as Orinthia to John Neville's King Magnus in Bernard Shaw's *The Apple Cart*, which was the culmination of a period working with directors like Donald McWhinnie (who directed *The Apple Cart* and also *There Will Be Some Changes Made* by Alun Owen which I was also in) and Minos Volonakis in Genet's *The Blacks*.

After that, casting became more cautious, not because one moved out of a particular age bracket but because the professionals involved in writing, producing and casting plays changed. We moved into a new age. Some of those people left the country or just dried up because of lack of support and understanding of what they were trying to do. Generally speaking, that was a very exciting time in British theatre, television and film, and I was part of that scene; it was something like a renaissance.

The next situation that really presented a rise and a challenge in my career was *Redemption Song* by Edgar White,

A Raisin in the Sun by Lorraine Hansbury, and James Baldwin's *The Amen Corner*. *A Raisin in the Sun* and *The Amen Corner* are very rare plays where black women are the central characters, especially when you consider that *A Raisin in the Sun* was written so long ago by an incredible young woman who was only twenty-five.

Then you have somebody like James Baldwin who could write a character like Sister Margaret in *The Amen Corner* and you think, 'How did he find this person?' Some of it, I think, was his father, although he put it into a woman's mouth. I think she was a mixture of both parents. There were echoes in it for me, but it remained a story – how she felt about getting on with her life; how, if the man isn't there, it's not the end of the world. At the same time, she was a real flesh and blood person. She felt pain, she didn't have all the answers from the start. She had to live through all the experiences in order to find those answers and some of them weren't right, like thinking that in creating this life for yourself you have to go down just one road, which is what she did. She shut everything out and plunged into religion – and that, too, became an empty shell because it was just covering up a lot of unresolved feelings.

It was very like a Greek tragedy. You saw the rise of the woman and then her fall. You saw everybody turning against her, her disintegration, her son leaving and then, at last, her realization that she gave up her life for nothing, really. She hears what life has been trying to tell her all this time when she says, how is she going to love God if she can't love her brethren. But for God you can substitute anything. How do you create this incredible life for yourself if you can't see where you are? She was aiming for some life that had nothing to do with human beings but with a belief in omnipotence. Attractive though it is, you've got to live in this world, live right here.

The thing that impressed me most and why I wanted to play her was the fact that she fell apart. That was a lesson I wanted people to watch. That kind of religiosity bordering on mania is no good for anybody, it doesn't solve any problems. It was good for me to play it because it confirmed my Buddhism. She was opting out, living in fear of some omnipotent being, in fear and guilt, whereas Buddhism for me is about who you are, who you're dealing with, where you are *now*. *Everything* that happens comes from one's own life, either in this existence or a past one. You are responsible for changing what is negative in your life.

There was a time when if I wasn't working it meant that I wasn't living fully. Now I no longer feel dead if I'm not working because my life has become bigger. It's about living with people, about my neighbour next door, my family. Those things were always there, but it's just more balanced for me now. I can relate to them with as much energy as I do anything else, although I still have the stage thing, it hasn't watered that down.

Acting is my job and I want to do it for as long as I possibly can. But if I couldn't work any more, it wouldn't be the end of the world for me now. It would mean that my life has simply moved into some other place – on, or sideways – because all life is change. In 1988, I came to this realization. Actually, this happened well before but, in 1988, I thought, 'I've had enough. I really cannot play another delinquent's mother, another black mother's mother, another depressed black lady with problems'. That's all that was happening. People are so short-sighted.

I've always gone to interviews feeling I'm going to sit down and have a wonderful talk with this person and that's going to be *it*. Getting the job is another thing. At least this one thing is complete. Then I look at the script and within two seconds of starting to read it, I *know* that I'm not going to do it and that I would like to transmit to that person that I don't want to do it. And when I hear they don't want me I'm very pleased! Going for the interview is still very important because if I don't do it, if I don't refuse that job, that person will never begin to understand that there's possibly something *wrong* with that job. Saying *no* is also a responsibility, but you're only saying no to one person. The terrifying thing is you wait nine months on the dole and it's the same job that comes up after that.

So after *The Amen Corner*, I thought, 'right, enough'. Then something came up. It was just doing an episode in a television series, maybe half an hour, doing four or five lines. I was desperate for work, I was extremely depressed, and I thought, 'Well, it's only a few days, they're paying very well'. But I had to say no. I'd been signing on for a long time and I thought, 'Maybe this is the time for me to go and do some studies'. I thought I'd do American Studies at Middlesex Poly, but the course was full. I tried Performance Arts, and that was full. Then there was a sit-in so I couldn't see anybody.

I was beginning to get the same feelings of panic as I had about the thing that I was leaving, and I thought, 'Wait a minute, this is where I came in, I cannot have this'. So I thought, 'Just let go, get down and start to really concentrate on your practice', because the whole thing of practising is being willing to change your situation and really change your life.

Within forty-eight hours this job on *Desmond's* came up. Now the question is, does *Desmond's* compare with the idea of a three-year degree course? No, it doesn't, because with *Desmond's* I am doing my job and, first and foremost, I have to be working if I'm to be fulfilling something in my working life. So that is *Desmond's* place.

I see this as a chance for me to arrange my life. I shall earn more money than I've earned on anything before. That's not because I'm going to earn a fortune, it's because I've earned so little altogether in the past. There are roles that have been denied to me. I'd like to play Madame Arkadina in *The Wild Duck*, for example. That is not to say it's not going to happen. I think it will because one's role or one's mission in life is also to stay in this business long enough to create a working situation where it will be credible to cast a black person.

There is a lot of pressure. Sometimes it's like being a welfare worker. That's what I've been doing, welfare work, since I started this business. Sometimes, it's absolute hell. You get all the nasty flak; as they say in America, 'whatever's going down, you get it'. You gotta stay with it. It takes a lot of courage and compassion, but I do stick with it because of the challenge. It's fulfilling. It's not necessarily about achieving for its own sake, but about turning situations over and being in a time when what you did made a positive difference to the society you lived in, and gave encouragement to other people in a similar situation to your own.

Having a child didn't conflict with my work, it just was very hard to do. How do you get to classes when you've got a child to look after? How do you get to learn the script? I used to type books to earn extra money. I did a lot of typing in my time. I used to work in a secretarial agency, typing stencils, rolling off scripts. It was frustrating enough but it was fun because I worked a lot with film companies. It got so that acting was a part-time thing and typing scripts was my job! There were all these lovely people, though – out of work performers – quite a lot struggling. You had a comradeship in your struggle as you do with other black artists – the ones who've come through it, because a lot fell by the wayside. It was hard to witness some of the falling. I mean, brains twisted, suicides, the lot.

In 1973, I came to the lowest point in my life and career with the realization that as long as I'm in this country and as long as I'm in this job, I will *never* realize my potential, as I know it, as I feel it. That was a shocking realization. I thought, 'What is there left to live for if that's what I know is going to be?' And then I thought, 'Maybe there's other things I have to do.' I mean, with whatever one accomplishes, in whatever small way, it is a contribution, it's going to make a difference.

It's not a compromise, it's something stronger than compromise. It's coming to understand that your life is bigger than the situation you're in. If you can come out of that, those obstacles, they become growth rings. And I came through, didn't I?

JULIA McKENZIE

'A lot of people are closet musical performers'

Born Enfield, Surrey. Trained Guildhall School of Music.

A wonderfully versatile musical, comedy and dramatic performer, Julia McKenzie is the leading interpreter of Stephen Sondheim in this country, having appeared in no less than four of his musicals – *Promises, Promises*, *Company*, *Follies* and *Into the Woods*, as well as the entertainment about his music, *Side By Side By Sondheim* with Millicent Martin, David Kernan and Ned Sherrin which, after the West End, went on to storm Sondheim's own citadel in New York. She also starred in the two musical revues, *Cole* and *Cowardy Custard* (about Cole Porter and Noël Coward).

Many will probably associate her more with the role of the ex-patriate wife, Hester in the TV sitcom *Fresh Fields* (which begat the current series, *French Fields*) and which made her Viewers Favourite Comedy Performer in 1985, 1986 and 1989.

She has also proved to be a superb exponent of Alan Ayckbourn's comic-tragedies, culminating in her award-winning role as Susan in his *Woman in Mind* (*Evening Standard* Best Actress and London Critics' Circle awards in 1986). She also added a fine satirical edge to the role of Pauline Collins's neighbour in the film *Shirley Valentine*.

Other stage highlights include Ayckbourn's *The Norman Conquests*, Richard Harris's *Outside Edge*, the musical *On the Twentieth Century*, and especially her performance as Miss Adelaide in the National Theatre's *Guys and Dolls* (with a now-famous cast which included Julie Covington, Ian Charleson and Bob Hoskins), which won her the Variety Club and SWET Best Actress awards.

She made her directorial début with Richard Harris's top-class comedy *Stepping Out*, followed in 1989 by *Steel Magnolias* by Robert Harling.

She is married to American actor, Jerry Harte, and they live in Surrey.

I'm not a fully blown actress because I can't do Shakespeare. I've had no formal training. As a child, I always wanted to act but didn't know how to go about it, and thirty years ago it was harder to begin than it is now. So, I gave up all ideas of doing it. I was going to teach French and was accepted at teacher training college, although I was always acting in the school productions. I was a real show-off.

One school speech day, just before I left, I sang a solo in the school choir and the county music adviser was there. He came round afterwards and said, 'I'll give you a scholarship for that voice'. I thought, 'This is the way in.'

The way in was four years' operatic training and at that time they made you do second study of a musical instrument. So, when I could have been doing acting classes, I was forced to do piano. All the time my nose was pressed up against the glass of the Drama Department. I used to get on their nerves and they would say, 'Go away, singers can't act. You can't come in here.'

So although I was close to it I still couldn't get in and I knew that my heart was in acting and not singing. I just happened to have a voice. My parents were 100 per cent behind me. My mother has a beautiful voice – hers is far superior to mine, even to this day, and she's seventy-eight.

When I left Guildhall, the first jobs that I could get were musical jobs because that's what I had been trained for, but *all* the time I kept pushing for drama. Occasionally, I managed to get rep jobs so that I could try and learn my craft that way.

I'm starting a new job – playing The Witch in Sondheim's *Into the Woods*. All right, it's a musical, but I've just been out and bought two books on acting. I do this *every* single time. I go out and buy books on it, read four chapters and think, 'I know about that, so that's all right'! It's a very odd process you have to go through. You hang by a slender thread all the time. I get a part and I think, 'Yes, I can do that.' Then I read it again, after I've taken it, and think, 'I can't do it, I won't be able to do this one' – and everything in the world gets put up against *not* doing it. It's ridiculous.

I've been a workaholic, but I've just taken six months off. I tell you it's going to have to be *some* part and *some* thing to get me out now! I have discovered the garden. I've just loved it, but maybe because I know I've a year's work to come back to! I really can't afford to give up work but, if I could, I'm beginning to think I wouldn't mind. I've been working thirty years and for a good eighteen of those it was really uphill. My family were not rich. My father was a works accountant in Enfield. I don't think he ever earned more than £1,000 a year in his life and my ma used to be a shop assistant to help with the money. So, to actually do what I like doing and to be paid very well for it now is just amazing. I can't get over it.

Side By Side By Sondheim is perhaps the show that made it for me, although I had been in *Company* before that in 1972. I took over, so nobody ever knew. I'd done a lot of musicals in London, but I'd either been understudying a leading lady, doing small parts or takeover parts. That never bothered me but nobody ever believes that. I loved the work and was delighted to get such parts, albeit the second time round. It's only after you do it the first time round that you think, 'Oh yes, this is quite different'!

Side By Side By Sondheim was like scaling the north face of the Eiger every night. You'd take a deep breath and think, 'Here we go!' Sondheim really asks a great deal of his performers. He makes both emotional and technical demands. A good vocal technique allied to acting ability. It must be like doing Shakespeare, because with the beauty and music of the language, you have to raise your sights every performance just to be equal to the material, let alone trying to interpret it. A big challenge – and never, *ever* boring.

I probably offend a lot of people because my vocal technique is not perfect. But my voice works for me and it stays healthy eight times a week, so I don't bother about it. Normally, when I'm doing a show, I do about twenty minutes' warm-up at about eleven o'clock in the morning and then, before the show, I do about ten minutes' physical warm-up.

Sondheim is such a superb dramatist that he even gives you the right thinking time, musically, for the next thought. His accompaniment always echoes the state that your body is in at that moment. He's brilliant. If you get just one Sondheim role in your lifetime, you're lucky. I shall have had four, with The Witch, so I count myself the most fortunate of performers.

Ayckbourn's *The Norman Conquests* was my first play in the West End, although I was second cast. The next time round, Ayckbourn gave me the first cast in *Ten Times Table*. I wasn't any good in it and I started to think, 'Is it that I can only follow people in parts?' Then I did an Ayckbourn on television called *Absent Friends* and I knew I was right for that. Alan saw me in that and gave me *Woman in Mind*.

With Ayckbourn, you find the character, and then you just follow his punctuation. If you follow that, the laugh comes. If you put a comma or a full stop in the wrong place, you don't get the laugh. The laughs come in the most unexpected places, usually from character.

There's no doubt that Ayckbourn's pinned down a lot of what makes up the fabric of English suburbia. Strangely enough, his plays are very big in Germany. I was relatively inexperienced for *Woman in Mind* and the enormity of the role preyed on me rather more than the role itself. I never left the stage and the success or failure of the evening rested on my shoulders despite the wonderful cast around me. If the central character isn't right, it doesn't mean anything.

I think actors always play out some aspect of their personality. There was certainly something of me in Susan. If that night hadn't happened when the music adviser gave me the scholarship, I could have had an entirely different life. I could well have married the local vicar, like Susan, got bogged down in her sort of life and tried to rise above it through humour. Her problem was one of frustration but I think it was also very menopausal too. Things got very blown up in her mind because of the time-of-life. I certainly based Susan very much on that. She had almost permanent PMT! I felt the whole play was about that.

I think women, in that state, can be very much on the brink of mental illness. I support two charities. One is Research into Ageing and the other one is the Mental Health Foundation. Perhaps this is because I think I'm just a step away from both! The menopause is a great period of loss for a woman. It's a time when she's losing so many things in her life: her looks, her womanhood – what she thinks is her womanhood – her children. A lot of women lose their husband. I think there was a great deal of truth about that in *Woman in Mind*. Plays about the male menopause, now they're just a bit jokey, aren't they? They seem to go back to boyhood and they'll have a little affair and that'll be all right because it's the male menopause.

Woman in Mind was an *enormous* learning process for me, not only from what I learnt from Alan, but from playing that size of part. I don't want to play small parts now. It's absolutely terrifying but, when you start to crack it, the sense of achievement and power is *tremendous*.

This is the thing about performing in the big parts. Most people think, 'It's only two and a half hours, that's all it is', but it's two and a half hours of concentration and most people find it difficult to concentrate for ten minutes. That's what wipes you out. When you *physically* go through those motions every night, it actually does something to the body, and the body says, 'Hey, hang on, this isn't right', and it goes sideways on you. It's very odd. I played Susan for seven and a half months and I was pretty ill at the end of it. My husband said I was very difficult to live with. I was very despondent and very tired all the time, because some of it had rubbed off on me.

I think *Woman in Mind* was the hardest play. The hardest musical was something called *On the 20th Century* which was like singing *Traviata* eight times a week. When I came off, I literally used to sit in the chair speechless. I was absolutely spent. Fortunately, for me, it didn't run for long.

I'm hoping I'll be able to keep my voice for a long while yet but, as I get older, my breathing isn't quite what it was. I have to work harder because my voice doesn't respond as it did even though I don't smoke at all – occasionally I'll borrow somebody's cigarette at a party – and I'm off the red wine because it makes your voice go down into your boots.

At the moment, I'm awfully pleased with myself! I've just started to exercise because I suddenly realized I was very unfit. I've always had a weight problem, basically because I'm greedy and I like my food. I thought, 'If I'm going to play this Witch in *Into the Woods*, there's an awful lot of body bending and I'm always putting my hip or my back out. I need some strength.' For the last six months I've been going to a body-conditioning studio and working out twice a week and it's made me much stronger.

When you've done musicals, as far as the acting world is concerned, you're a second-class citizen. I know a lot of straight actors who are closet musical performers! In America, somebody like me is called 'a triple threat'. They see it as a positive thing. In Britain, they say, 'She spreads it too thinly, can't do it all.'

I remember years ago I did a demo disc for a musical. After the recording, the director ran over to me and the other singers and said, 'Oh terrific, oh Julia that was so good', and I said, 'Thank you, may I have the chance to audition for this part?' And he said: 'Oh my dear, no, you sing far too well to ever be able to act' – and that truly is the attitude. There are a few people who have broken through the barrier like Dennis Quilley and Imelda Staunton. I hope I have, too, and I think getting the drama award for *Woman in Mind* helped.

I started off my acceptance speech with an old Noël Coward line. It was actually the telegram that he sent to Gertrude Lawrence on her first straight play: 'Legitimate at last, won't mother be pleased'! That's exactly what I felt like because it *is* hard. The first time you get an award, it's lovely – not to be ignored – but they don't really mean very much because there are at least six or seven wonderful perform-ances a year in the West End. It's all a bit silly and because of the media coverage and because it's actually cheap tele-vision, it's been rather spoiled now.

Television and film have made actors go a bit soft. It's a very easy way to earn money and working on TV certainly puts one's rate up. So suddenly, people aren't willing to commit to theatre for any length of time any more. I do sitcom and I don't have to apologize for it. It pays a lot and subsidizes my work in the theatre. I'm not saying I get a pittance in the theatre. I don't now – but for years I did and I don't know how young actors manage to keep going with a family and mortgage commitments.

Sitcom is a genre entirely of its own. It's very *exact*. The camera crew have to know where you are and you have to know where you are, within millimetres. There's a studio audience just the other side of the cameras but I think on the thin spots they do pipe in a bit of taped laughter.

I've also done commercials. Actors say to me, 'Oh commercials, you mustn't.' I'm sorry, I think it is *all* part of earning a living, I see nothing wrong in it. I don't see that acting is so noble a profession that you can't do the other things that let you earn money in order to survive. I wouldn't do commercials for certain products and I wouldn't do political campaigns. I'm a very strong believer – and this will probably bring the wrath of God about my head – that theatre people should not be seen to be political. I do not want anybody to vote the way I vote just because they happen to see me in *Fresh Fields*. And they do, you know; they think, 'Oh Hester's voted this way, well I shall do that'. I really wish well-known faces would leave it alone.

I try not to be aware of the power that comes from television because being well known is something I am not very good at coping with. I tend to wear dark glasses and hats and I'm not very good at being approached. If I go to the supermarket in jeans, with no makeup, and somebody comes up and says, 'Oh you're not as fat as you look on the box', I think, 'I should have put makeup on because they'll think I'm a frump'. I have to say to myself, 'What the hell do you care what they think. It's fine, don't worry about it.'

I suppose, because the work I do is public, I have a responsibility. Perhaps sometimes I don't rise to that responsibility as much as I should. The public have certain images of television personalities and maybe one shouldn't disappoint them. But I do get very incensed when they think they can say anything to me. Today, a cab driver said, 'Hello Hester' and, trying to be bright, I said 'Hello'. And he said, 'That's a small car for you to be driving isn't it?' For ten seconds, I was furious: 'What does he think I'm going to

209

drive – a Rolls Royce? What's the matter with my car?' It's so silly. Then I thought, 'What *are* you going on about, calm down, it doesn't matter.'

I say to people, 'Acting's like being a plumber – that's what I do. I come with my little bag of tricks and I fit a few pipes together and I make the sink work – it's a trade.' What I can't cope with is the glamour that goes with it. I'd love the utopia of getting big parts, having lovely times in big parts and nobody knowing about it!

To me acting is only *re*acting. With *Guys and Dolls*, for example, I found Miss Adelaide simply by reacting to what Bob Hoskins gave me. She'd simply wrapped her life around Nathan. I put the high heels and the wig on, got the accent and just followed him around. When he left and Trevor Peacock took over, I had to rediscover Adelaide because there was a different chemistry between us.

That's the only way I can make it work. It has to come from inside. I don't think the classical repertoire is my bag really. I wouldn't mind having a go if I was protected with a really good director who would help me if I was in trouble – and I would be! I think I could have a go at something, maybe not Lady Bracknell but perhaps Mrs Malaprop. The classics have been done so wonderfully that I'm a bit scared to try, so I stick mainly to new plays.

I get mostly suburban women parts but they're all different people to me. This Witch I'm going to do is quite a departure for me, which I'll enjoy. People could say I just play the one thing. Maybe it's because I wasn't brave enough when I was younger, and didn't take the chances. Now I'm more established, I don't know that I'm brave enough to risk rocking the boat. I don't want to fail now, I failed enough in the first unsuccessful seventeen years, which is a long while.

I can be difficult. There is a point past which I will not go and it's when people presume too much. I have had times quite recently when a male actor has dominated rehearsal time to such an extent that no time is left over for others at all, and I've put my foot down. Strangely enough, that's only since I've started directing. You learn an awful lot about yourself when directing.

The two things I've directed, *Steel Magnolias* and *Stepping Out*, were both by men, Richard Harris and Robert Harling. Both write well about women. Richard Harris is a friend of the family. He always sends me his new things before they go to his agent. *Stepping Out* came along and I said, 'It's very funny, Richard, in a sort of Beryl Cook way. The only thing is, you must get a woman to direct it. She will bring out things only women know about. Those women behaved for you because you were in the corner. (Richard had sat in on the women's dancing classes that the play is centred around.) Women are entirely different when they are on their own.' There aren't many lady comedy directors, and I heard myself saying, 'Oh God, I'll do the bloody thing!' It happened by accident, but the script had played like a film in my head so I didn't have any trepidation.

The only thing I was worried about was finding a platform for myself as a director, with women I knew. Directing, for a woman, is difficult, but both plays had all-female casts. That was easier because I like women very much and I feel happier directing them. I have a rapport with them and I don't much want to take on male actors. Women in rehearsal will often let things go past and be fairly self-effacing simply to get on with rehearsal in the time and give a positive flow to the day. We'll all chuck ideas in but I'll have the last vote. It seems to work. Women will be reasonable.

The male ego in rehearsal is something else. I don't know whether they think it's not a job for a grown-up man or something, but some men have to throw a great deal of flak

211

up in rehearsals. As an actress I know how to deal with that, but I wouldn't know how to deal with it as a director. I'm still a coward about actually having a showdown.

I think, with experience, there's a shorthand between a director and an actor. When you're younger, you might have a discussion. Gradually, as you get older, you play it your way. I think most actresses would say the same.

The parts I've played have all been favourites in a way. I have to hold myself back from being very emotional on the last night because I'm saying goodbye to the character. I get very easily moved to tears and I have to stop thinking, 'This is the last time I'm going to play this'. The last night of *Side By Side* in Britain was like we were going out to win the Whiteman Cup. People came on stage and we all joined hands and sang 'Auld Lang Syne'. We all wallowed for ages, it was lovely.

The thing about acting is that it's all in the air, there's not an awful lot to show for it. I *love* to act but of course it's only left in people's memories and that gets distorted. I wish I'd got something to leave behind. I suppose it's because I don't have any children. I was a single child so the McKenzies are going to burn out. All they'll have left of me will be films like *The Belles of St Trinians* and things I wish I'd never done!

That's the disappointment: you feel you've devoted your life to doing something ephemeral. In the end, the characters all get away. I think acting in the theatre is pretty much gossamer because everything you devote time and energy to just disappears.

HARRIET WALTER

'Which would you rather – quantity or quality?'

Born London. Trained LAMDA.

Harriet Walter first came to prominence playing Ophelia opposite Jonathan Pryce's *Hamlet* at the Royal Court, having worked with some of the most influential fringe companies of the early eighties: John McGrath's 7:84 company, Paines Plough, Joint Stock, and in several Royal Court productions: Caryl Churchill's *Cloud Nine*, the Irish version of Chekhov's *The Seagull*, and Julia in Aphra Behn's *The Lucky Chance* (with Alan Rickman), which launched the Women's Playhouse Trust.

Her Imogen in Bill Alexanders's 1987 RSC production of *Cymbeline* confirmed for one critic that she was 'destined for greater things' while her performance as Masha in John Barton's production of *Three Sisters* drew some ecstatic responses: '[with] her pale, iconic face and burning, dark eyes, she presses her body as though every bone aches with waste' said the *Observer*'s Michael Ratcliffe. She was equally praised in the same year for her portrayal of the mother, imprisoned in one of Stalin's camps in John Berger and Nella Bielski's *A Question of Geography*. She's since appeared in *The Possessed*, directed by the Russian director, Yuri Lyubimov, and in 1990 scored more critical success at the RSC as the Duchess in Webster's *The Duchess of Malfi*.

On television, she made a huge impact as the young girl in Ian McEwan's *The Imitation Game* (with Bill Paterson); also as the businessman's wife held hostage in Channel 4's Northern Ireland thriller, *The Price* (with Peter Barkworth) and as Harriet Vane in the BBC's Dorothy L. Sayers Mysteries trilogy (1986).

Films include *The Good Father* with Antony Hopkins, and Louis Malle's *Milou en mai* in which her 1968 hippy-actress was a delightful and affectionate spoof on the flavour of those times.

In 1991, she appears in the BBC's *The Men's Room* adapted from the novel by Ann Oakley.

She lives in London.

I more or less decided to act round about the time of my parents' divorce. I was twelve and at boarding school. I can remember the moment of walking on to the stage in the school gym in what was a pretty small comic cameo, tentatively saying my first line and then an experience of holding on to a taut line of connection with the audience, a bit like controlling a kite. Bit by bit, as I plopped in my one-liners and built on the laughter, I felt the magic of what I now know to be timing. It was something terribly instinctive and it brought the house down. I've probably never been as good since! It got back to me that the headmistress had said, 'that girl's a natural actress' and I got this standing ovation when I went into the school dinner at the end of it. That clinched it. From that moment on, it became my identity.

I didn't connect it at all with upheavals at home but, looking back on it, it did provide some kind of an outlet for various things. I thought and still feel the theatre is a place where you can go through crises safely, express a lot of emotions you're not allowed to express domestically.

At school, I primarily discovered that I could make people laugh, which is a bit paradoxical because I'm not known as a comic actress. I remember being very shy and reticent at six and seven. When the teachers were dishing out the big parts, I hid under the desk, but when they said, 'Who wants to have a very, very small part?', I put my hand up. I couldn't bear not to be in it at all. Looking back, I realize that, because I secretly wanted to do it so well, I didn't dare do it because I didn't want to be bad. I was this big mixture of being terribly shy and very competitive, in the sense of never being quite satisfied with myself. Whatever the roots, I feel very driven as a person.

It had been mapped out for me to go to university but I ducked off the path and aimed at drama school instead. I don't, in any way, regret not having been to university.

Whatever brain or analytical powers I've got have been extremely useful and served me well in the theatre because I've certainly learned to think, inquire and research if the part requires it. I'm a bit of a magpie. Most actors are forced to be, I think. That's suited me better than getting locked into one area of study. I feel it has a certain end, namely to perform a play.

My parents have always been very supportive and were pleased I knew so clearly what I wanted to do. I'd never been brought up to think in terms of a career or earning my living for myself. Being paid for something I was interested in was viewed as a bonus. My background may have been upper middle class but it was also quite cosmopolitan. It certainly wasn't philistine. My parents taught me how to fit in and how to be socially adept.

Funnily enough, I didn't have it in my mind particularly to be a classical actress. I was thinking more of the screen because it was the minutiae of things that I was interested in – things going on behind the eyes. A camera lens focuses in; in that sense, you're more passive. It's a more 'feminine' medium whereas the stage requires a lot of energy, dynamism, initiative – putting it out. It's an extrovert sort of medium. I would, very much, have defined myself as an introvert at that stage and so, I think, the camera appealed to me.

I also thought that I could lose myself in film, get carried away as I did as a cinema spectator. But I was to be disillusioned.

At the age of nine or ten, I'd go down to Bray Studios to watch my uncle, Christopher Lee, making Hammer horror movies and I discovered that Dracula's castle was really made of papier mâché. In fact, I've discovered in the few films I have made that you're much less likely to lose yourself in a film. It's so artificial. You have to be so technical and aware of what's going on. It looks like the camera just catches you haphazardly while you're in the middle of doing something, but it's so repeated, so set up. The illusion of spontaneity is painstakingly and artificially contrived. It's the most self-conscious medium you could think of. So that was a bit of a disappointment. I really thought I could go in to the screen and lose myself and become somebody else. I think that was the attraction as a child. It's play. Being in the theatre is just an extension of that, but it's serious play and it has a duty with it which is to take a whole lot of other people along with you. You've got to make things real for them.

I didn't idolize Shakespeare or have any great love of poetry at school. They've all come later. I see myself very much as having been a tortoise in the tortoise and hare race. I got rejected by about five drama schools and finally got into LAMDA. My talent wasn't very up-front and I wasn't very good at presenting myself. But LAMDA saw some glimmer behind my diffidence.

I went to drama school relatively late, at twenty. I'd lived a bit and I'd got politicized in quite dramatic ways since leaving school and had discovered social guilt. No one at LAMDA shared my background and I tried to keep it hidden. I was terribly self-conscious about my class and, like a lot of my generation, wanted to lose the outward trappings, tone down my accent, that sort of thing, in order to bypass those prejudices that I felt would get in the way of my connecting with people.

I've since learned that a lot of people went through that – and a lot of people decided to go the other way – but that was the choice I made and so drama school was a very strange, exploratory time for me. At times, I felt quite fraudulent and ill at ease but I didn't want to be defined by my class or contextualized. I wanted to be this free being of the universe – a blank page, completely able to merge with any group of people. Of course, you can't. But that's what I aimed to do.

Actors are often called classless and my fellow students were going through other versions of this melting pot so we'd all meet somewhere in the middle. Because I'd had a good education in English and because my parents went to the theatre, I had no inferiority complex with regard to the classics, which I think definitely affected some people in my year. Instead, I felt dwarfed and threatened by regional culture, political theatre and modern, working-class drama. That's why I went immediately into community theatre because I've always treated the theatre and acting as a vehicle, a means of exploring bits of the world I was afraid of and would never normally come into contact with.

Eventually, through more and more demanding work, I've had to confront myself more honestly. It's partly to do with acting in plays by writers like Shakespeare and Chekhov. They require you to create something much closer to yourself, to dig more deeply. I suppose I started having to encounter what I really thought about things. I feel more able to do this because of the breadth of experience my tortoise-like journey through political and fringe theatre gave me. I'm sure that if I hadn't gone that roundabout route, I might easily have been limited to playing rich bitches on television.

When people talk about you being a feminist actress, it isn't that you say, 'Ah here's this part. Now as a feminist, I'm going to bend the interpretation, I've got to toe the right line.' It's simply that your experiences inform your vision and your choices. It's much more at gut level. Quite often, I've turned down parts because they don't appeal to me simply because I'm not interested in expressing that particular view of a woman.

*　　*　　*

I was in my early thirties after a longish stint at the RSC, when I was asked to play in the TV thriller, *The Price*, about a kidnap in Northern Ireland. I was very nervous, firstly because it meant greater exposure than I'd ever had but also I was wary of its political content or lack of it. I was being protective of some small reputation for political integrity which I flattered myself I had and didn't want to lose on such a public scale. A less precious actress might simply have leapt at it as a great part in a jolly thrilling series.

The Price was essentially a human drama, but it was set against the backdrop of the political situation in Ireland. I was worried that it was just exploiting that to 'up' the tension while dodging the Northern Ireland issue.

I actually turned it down at first but my agent insisted I talk to the writer before deciding. So I talked to him and expressed certain reservations. It wasn't that I thought it was ideologically unsound, it was just something that could have been treated badly or cheaply. I'd worked almost exclusively in the theatre where on the whole, like-minded people worked through some kind of rough consensus. And now here was the mighty TV machine, run by strangers. Once I'd agreed to jump on, I'd have to go where it was going.

My conversations with the writer reassured me, but I was finally swayed by a conversation with one of the Irish actors involved who had been brought up with first-hand experience of the Northern Ireland situation and was extremely politically aware. I thought, 'If they go along with this, who am I to complain?' I felt ignorant and didn't trust my own political instincts so I borrowed theirs. I now have a less overblown sense of the importance of my choices for anyone else but I still need to square what I do with my own conscience. I've had the luxury of working with people and on projects that I can feel totally committed to. I know what I value. So why throw that away?

Working in a big institution like the RSC, I certainly feel a thread that continues from schooldays when I liked fitting in and belonging and feeling necessary to something. I like feeling that the whole institution needs me to turn up at 7 o'clock to play my part. Some people get that feeling domestically, others at the office. I don't have a family expecting me to get up and make breakfast for them, so it's kind of displaced. To offset this rather dangerous tendency, I have a vagabond streak which doesn't like being pinned down. So I see-saw between institutionalization and being freelance and try to create an edge of danger within the safety of work.

If we have a sort of character makeup that's developed in childhood, I would have characterized mine as the younger sister syndrome, meaning that I followed and fitted in and obeyed and got a sense of satisfaction from doing that. But I could be sneakily subversive within that role and never take on responsibility or initiative. Then there comes the day when you suddenly realize you're not the youngest, you're no longer the-up-and-coming. There are younger people around who are feeling as frightened and as timid and unsure of themselves as you did and still do, but they don't think *you* do. So you've got to sort of come out of your little problem and take on a leadership role.

For me, there was an actual point at which I remember arguing with a director on behalf of some of the other members of the company who didn't feel they could argue. I hadn't done it out of any sense of duty. I'd done it because I felt very strongly about it. The theatre's a great leveller. You do feel still in touch with being lower down in the hierarchy because it isn't terrible stable as a hierarchy. You can be up one day and down the next. I identified with these people who were, I thought, being kept in the dark about something. I realized that when you're playing named parts of certain substantial weight, you're less substitutable than if you're carrying a spear, so you can risk sticking your neck out when somebody else can't.

It *is* difficult to acquire the sense of 'I've got a right to interrupt things here and put in my piece'. It has taken me a very long time. It's easier for me now at the RSC because I've got a track record and maybe they think I'm worth listening to. That's a bit nerve-wracking because suddenly I find everyone's shut up because it's me talking and they think I know what I'm talking about.

I'm still looking out to make sure it's all right. I think my conditioning is partly responsible for that, which makes me constantly look around the dining-room table, so to speak, to make sure everybody's got what they want: has he got the salt and do their glasses need filling? I certainly feel that in a rehearsal. Am I taking up too much time? Has so and so had their say? Am I taking too much out of the director's mouth and diminishing his authority?

I don't think it's a helpful attitude. It's inhibited me a lot to be so worried about everybody else and what they're thinking about. Over the years, I'm pleased to say, something else has taken over that is more forceful and more outspoken in that area of work.

By total contrast, last year, I did a French film, *Milou en mai*, directed by Louis Malle. I couldn't have been more of an outsider. It's a film about 1968 and I was playing an English woman who's married to a Frenchman and spending some time in their family house. I was playing a rather bimboesque actress from the Kings Road – the sort of person who'd have been in the background in *Georgie Girl* or *The Knack*, with mini-skirts and Cathy McGowan bangs.

The irony was that I was playing the sort of actress I'd happily avoided having to be, by virtue of having been born five or ten years later. If it had been in English, I might have thought the role not challenging enough and probably wouldn't have wanted to do it. But as it was in French and directed by Louis Malle, it was an adventure in itself and there was a sort of pioneering bit about it that completely outweighed the detraction of playing that particular character. Also, it was very lightly touched in. Compared to the gritty kind of thinking and getting to grips with a character that I'd been used to, this was like a butterfly on holiday.

In France, my track record counted for very little and, without my reputation to keep me warm, I had to swallow my pride and send my ego back on the plane for a couple of months. There are times when it's very relaxing to be almost invisible and just explore and be curious – and leave behind this person you've created, this intricately presented person.

On the other hand I felt disarmed – literally deprived of my armoury. Dressed and bewigged as I was, out of my context and speaking a foreign language, I was often taken on face value as sweet and simple and slightly dumb.

I felt insulted sometimes but I went along with it. Acting in film, you really need context more than anything. You need to know the story that's being told and who's clipping the frame. You can't go against that. With *Milou*, there was no reference to why she was who she was or what she was. The film didn't concern itself with her. She was an ingredient, a colour, a dash of spice and I was happy to be that because I trusted the context. I was not prevented from putting in tiny touches and details of my own but there was little of my own experience that I could make relevant to that part.

In some ways, I've had very little experience of direct, raw life and yet, in another way, you confront quite a lot of things through the work. The characters can work on you in such a way that you can actually glean their wisdom. In *A*

Question of Geography, the character I played had been in Stalin's camps. Now that is unimaginable to me. I can't expect to get near it or feed any of *my* experience into it. But the process can go the other way and you can learn to understand the character's attitude. That requires a very sure-footed playwright, mind you – you're dependent on their insight, usually a male insight. Even the greatest playwrights, being men, force you to respond against your natural inclinations. For example, they are forever making their heroines weep at the drop of a hat! Even, the Duchess of Malfi, having told someone forcefully to get lost is told by her husband, 'do not weep'. Who says I was weeping?

Often, on the face of it, one is playing a passive victim – for example, the Duchess of Malfi – but with playwrights like Shakespeare and Webster the actual language and the reaching for it become muscular, powerful activities.

There are still not enough parts for women. I don't just say that on behalf of actresses slavering for meaty roles, but as a female member of the audience wanting to see a truer reflection of the world. It's true that the raising of feminist consciousness has led to more plays about women but it isn't just about having *a* woman centre stage. That provides a star vehicle but not a healthy population.

Look down any cast list from the *dramatis personae* of a Shakespeare play to any drama in the *TV Times* and just do a male versus female head count. Granted, a lot of the men may be carrying spears – and there may only be three good parts for men – but they're working, earning, doing it.

It is even harder for women as directors because there are fewer chances for them. Nobody is a good director over-night, despite what some people think. Trevor Nunn did some productions that were slammed but people forget that. You only learn your craft through actually doing it, in directing more than anything else. It's a very practical thing and involves knowing and learning about people and the acting process as well as knowing an awful lot about the play you're directing. Women get far, far less chance to practise and when they do suddenly get given a chance, all eyes go on them. They probably haven't directed a play of that complexity for four years whereas a man's done one a year. If it fails in any way, they've got to climb right up the ladder again. How are we going to develop these people if we don't give them chances?

A director has to be a step ahead of the game, provoke, listen and watch and guide a production towards its fulfilment. She or he has also got to be a social person, someone who knows how to communicate with lots of different individuals and bring out each one of them, like the best teachers can. That is part of the process, you can't go in as a neutral, asexual being. You're going to be received as a woman or a man director and that's going to set up whatever reverberations that sets up and make your job easier or more difficult.

So you think, 'Well, women are usually better at being sensitive to your needs and picking up what you want to say and making sure everybody's getting a look in, not just the main parts.' So I don't understand why there aren't more of them as directors. There doesn't seem to be anything about their makeup that stops them being able to do it. So we come to the issue of power and authority which still seem to be more acceptable in a man than a woman.

We've had so little experience of women directors, we're still testing them out. But then we test all directors out because so much depends on them. Are they going to liberate me or choke me? Am I going to be able to communicate with them? Are they going to listen to me? These are the kind of anxieties you have when you enter a rehearsal room.

I've worked with far too few women directors. I've only worked with two or three at the most and all the individual directors I've worked with, male or female, are so different from one another. I couldn't say all males were like this or all females were like that, although a lot of people want you to say that. In my experience, it doesn't fall quite as easily as that.

Aphra Behn's *The Lucky Chance*, which I did with the Women's Playhouse Trust, didn't quite match my expectations either. My wishful thinking had wanted her women characters to be frightfully liberated role models but it just brought home to me that any writer is part of their surroundings and society. The heroines were very celebratory and spirited – celebrating whatever rights they'd got and turning them to their own use. There was this wonderful division of purpose whereby it was understood you could marry an older man for security and status at the same time as knowing that you could, legitimately, have lovers on the side. But even Behn didn't mention anything about bearing children – the thing that burdens women most. The result of all these antics could be childbirth, and childbirth could mean death. But that is excluded from the conversations.

I was surprised that Behn was as like her male counterparts as she was. That, I suppose, is what she was trying to prove – that she was up with them and that she had her own individual voice. The whole enterprise was just so extraordinary, learning that there was this pocket of time where these women playwrights flourished, and to learn that that had somehow been historically 'not counted'. I'm very conscious, now, that the recording of things historically is dependent on their ability to be encapsulated in some slogan. If you can define something clearly in words, then it stands a chance of remaining on the records.

* * *

I don't really have favourite roles but, if you ask me, I think Masha in *Three Sisters* is my all-time favourite. I've played her twice. I think I've probably finally exhausted her but maybe never quite . . . If you'd asked me ten years ago, I would have said that Nina in *The Seagull* was my favourite; there's something about Chekhov heroines that I love.

I did enjoy doing that woman in *The Price* a lot, too. It was very unlike anything I'd done, very meaty and with masses of variety in it – the most detailed work I'd done on film. Every scene presented a new challenge. It was a five-month crash course in filming. Then I did *The Imitation Game*, the BBC play, written by Ian McEwan. That just dropped out of the sky and seemed like it had been written for me.

The rebound, in terms of work, in my experience, takes a while to come through – more like a year later. The seeds for what you're likely to do later are laid now. Maybe this year I'm laying the seeds for something I might do in four years' time.

There was a wonderful time around the mid-eighties when I was getting very contrasting jobs that had all been arrived at from totally different sources and were going in various directions. I'd love to keep that going.

From where I'm standing now, I don't feel smug about how fortunate and privileged I've been. Rather, I get very angry at the unused talent I see around me. I can honestly say that whether or not I play Cleopatra in four years' time matters far less to me than that there should be a broad-based and prolific theatre and film industry that is appreciated and not insultingly underfunded.

BERYL REID

'How have you been this century?'

Born in Hereford of Scottish parents and educated in Manchester.

Beryl Reid is one of Britain's best loved performers, with a career spanning all aspects of entertainment, from variety and revue to the National Theatre. In the fifties, her radio work, especially the creation of the two Birmingham characters, Monica and Marlene, made her a household name.

Since then, her wonderful gift for comic characterization has leant itself to such contrasting roles as Kath in Joe Orton's *Entertaining Mr Sloane*, the Restoration classics – Mrs Candour and Lady Wishfor't in *School for Scandal* and *The Way of the World* – and George, in Frank Marcus's *The Killing of Sister George*.

She has continued to appear regularly on television alternating it with work in pantos, radio, and variety – she stopped the show in the Jubilee Concert as *Burlington Bertie* – and with major appearances in Shaw, Shakespeare, Wedekind, Noël Coward, and musicals. On television, she has played both Grandma Mole in *The Secret Diary of Adrian Mole*, and starred alongside Alec Guinness in John Le Carré's *Tinker, Tailor, Soldier, Spy* and its sequel, *Smiley's People* (for which she was nominated for a Best Actress award).

One of the original 'Belles of St Trinians', her film work includes *The Killing of Sister George*, *Entertaining Mr Sloane*, *Psychomania* with George Sanders, *Joseph Andrews* and *Inspector Clouseau* with Peter Sellers.

Two autobiographies – *So Much Love*, and *The Cat's Whiskers*, were both bestsellers; she has also written a cookbook, *Beryl, Food and Friends*. In 1986, she was made an OBE. She lives in a delightful Thameside cottage in Surrey with her many and beloved cats.

I started on the stage in concert parties at £2 a week, doing a little turn and being in sketches. I was a dancer in 1936. I've had a very long career – I'm going to be seventy-one this year – but I don't feel it, that's the awful thing. I can't do everything I used to and I think, 'It must be because I'm getting older', but I still feel twelve inside. My brain is very active and my memory's still good which I think has a lot to do with not feeling old.

Acting didn't run much in the family. My brother was a scientist and my father was an auctioneer, valuer and estate agent when an estate agent was still a reputable thing to be. My mother had been a secretary to a solicitor. Scottish, very respectable. She was from Edinburgh, my father from Aberdeen. They never lost being Scottish although I was born in Hereford and my brother and I went to school in Manchester.

Mother loved the theatre. People didn't go on the stage in her young day, but she always encouraged me, although she never let me think I was any good: 'You're not bonnie; I don't suppose you'll get the job'. If anybody ever wanted to marry me, she'd say, 'I don't know what anyone sees in you, Beeryl'. Funnily enough, it never depressed me. She must have had some faith in me. She used to say, 'Don't forget, Beeryl, there's nothing you can't do.' I had so little knowledge then that I did think I could do a lot. I know now that I couldn't.

I left school when I was sixteen because there was no point in going on with it. I only ever wanted to go on the stage. My brother was the brilliant one. We were total opposites but I was very fond of him. On the phone, I'd say to him 'What do you think of that then?' There'd be silence at the other end. I'd say 'Are you there?' And he'd say 'Yes, I'm just giving it my consideration.' Now, I'd say anything. It may not be right, just my instinct at that moment. But actors live off that. They need to be able to work off each other quickly.

My mother sort of apologised later on: She said, 'I didn't realise that people were clever in different ways.' The only genuine gift I've got is being able to slip into accents – a bit of mimicry. When I was about four, I used to put my father's hat on and be Uriah Heep or something. I've never had any tuition. All I ever learned was dancing.

My career developed very slowly. I did variety for years. I used to do impressions, then I started telling a few jokes and then, eventually, at the Watergate Club in London (which is no longer in existence), I used to do funny sketches in late-night revue. I didn't write my own material but I could say to whoever was writing it, 'oh no, she wouldn't say that', because I'd already formed the character in my head. Or I'd say, 'I don't want to do that, I don't like it.' I got a name for being rather po-faced. I didn't want to do things that were rude just to be funny or because it rhymed. You know: 'If you want flagellation, try Charing Cross station'. It was an insight, I suppose, into what I eventually wanted to do.

When I was at the Watergate, I only got £1 a show but I knew that that was what I ought to try and do, to see if I liked it. I was doing sketches or a monologue, which was nothing like I'd ever done in variety where you come on as yourself, a bare person without a coathanger.

Revue in those days was wonderful. I remember doing one called *One to Another* at the old Lyric, Hammersmith with Patrick Wymark. I loved him; we worked a lot together. He'd come straight from Stratford. One night, he said, 'Have you noticed that if there are going to be some things cut out of the show, they don't actually tell you? You just go to the dressing room the next night and the clothes are missing.' I said, 'Yes, I have noticed that.' And he said, 'Another thing – you have to establish the characters quite quickly, don't you?' I said, 'Well, actually, ten seconds flat or get off.'

In 1944, I did a sixteen-week pantomime season at the Theatre Royal in Birmingham. I had very little responsibility in the theatre in those days – a little ugly sister, that kind of thing. I got fascinated by the Birmingham accent and especially a dresser who'd say, 'Goodnight each. My grandad you know, he was a bugger with the women, people used to refer to him as "the Balsal Heath stallion".' I thought, 'Oh I must remember all this.' Actually I didn't use it until eleven years later. I'd already been doing Monica, the schoolgirl character, for two years on the radio in a programme called *Educating Archie* with Peter Brough and his ventriloquist dummy, Archie. One day, I said to Brough, 'If I've got any sense at all, I ought to try another character as well as Monica.'

I tried a posh cockney character and people said, 'Oh, that's very good, it's just like Joyce Grenfell'. I thought, 'Well that's no good then, I want something completely different.' So I tried the Birmingham character. I got Ronnie Wolfe, who wrote the Monica material for me, to write Marlene and I told him I wanted her to be just like the kids were. Whatever they wore, I wore. I always dressed up for the radio shows because all those Sunday lunchtime programmes – *Take It From Here*, *Life with the Lyons*, *Round the Horn* – had studio audiences. It was peak listening time.

I think I'm one of the very last people to have become well known through radio. I stayed with *Educating Archie* for four years and it was a big step up for me. I loved it. I still love radio. In fact, I did a programme just last week about my favourite comics. It was a wonderful afternoon. I had more fun than anybody. I loved watching Jacques Tati, too, in *Monsieur Hulot's Holiday* over Easter. You don't see anything like it now because he was a clown. All the people I've admired and learnt a lot from were clowns.

I learned a great deal from a Scot called Dave Willis.

Nobody from this side of the border knows him. I did 427 sketches with him in the *Half Past Eight Show* and never had a word written down. We did five or six different sketches every week and every week we changed them. I used to say, 'Dave, what are we going to do next week?' And he'd say 'Weel, you come on. And then you say so and so and so and so. And then I'll come on and then we do a wee bit of chat, and some patter' and then he told me the tag line. That's all I ever had. I had to go on and just busk it. It did me so much good.

It's hard to say who was the best comic I worked with, although I enjoyed Dave Willis very much. I got on well with most comics. But I also did a lot on my own. When I was working a lot with comics – I call that being a comic's labourer, being a 'feed' – they do try to keep you under. You're really a stooge because you've got to know how to get laughs for them. When I started getting laughs with straight lines, they got rather depressed.

Variety, revue, theatre – they're all totally different but that's what's so good for you. At one time, I was doing the Nurse in *Romeo and Juliet* and the German Mother in *Spring Awakening* at the National at the Old Vic, and every Sunday I went to Bournemouth and did two performances of Old Tyme Music Hall. Lovely, a bit of song and dance.

I've done so much work and I've got so much enjoyment from it. I've been very fulfilled. So I don't go grunting and groaning and saying, 'I don't think this is right.' I've said this to so many people: 'Don't argue with the director before you've tried it. If you've done it three times and you've found it's a dead loss and nothing to do with you, *then* have an argument and say, "I don't think it's anything to do with me". But give it a try. It might be something new for you.'

I'd say I'm quite a strong personality. But I'm blotting

paper for directors, if they're good. They're the only people who can have a general picture of what they want at the end of it all. I have a great regard for them, if they're nice.

John Dexter was really awful to me in *Gigi*. I said one day at rehearsal, 'If you ever speak to me like that again, in front of this cast who really quite like me, I shall get in the car and go home and I won't come back. And you'll have to explain to the management why I'm not there. It's nothing to do with me, it's your bad behaviour and your total lack of judgement about me.' Of course, on the opening night we had a great success. But I barred him from the theatre. I said, 'He must not be allowed into the theatre when I'm here. He's only going to upset me then I'll be in tears again and I can't do it.' The work is very creative so you're on a knife edge all the time.

I loved doing *Born in the Gardens* by Peter Nichols. She was such a marvellous character, Maude, a terrible old woman, with pink hair that you could see through – a very clever wig, just the way hair goes thin on top in older people. I think the character was based on Peter Nichols's mother because, on the opening night, she was saying very loudly in the bar, 'I do want you all to know that I'm not represented at all in this play, there's no one resembling me'.

I thought the things Peter wrote were so funny. Humour is, of course, very personal. Some things wear well. Tati wears well because the jokes are still funny. The secret of humour is that an audience can see you're in danger and if they really care about you as a character or a person, they don't want the thing to happen to you. But it's inevitable. They know you're going to fall into the pit, to get into a mess. And so people laugh, almost out of nerves.

I keep my ears and especially my eyes open. Even without knowing that I'm doing it, I could tell you exactly what somebody's wearing when they walk past me, and what shoes they've got on which affect their walking. Terrible isn't it? It's all stored up there somewhere.

Mrs Candour and Lady Wishfor't are wonderful characters to play, caricatures really. They're always trying to be frightfully grand, and trying to be sexy, because Wishfor't was Wish-For-It and she always wondered why they went after the younger ones. When she looks in the mirror and says, 'Oh my face is like an old peeled wall', it's because the base of the stuff they used for makeup was zinc.

I know all about that century now. If I've done any of those eighteenth-century characters, I've gone deeply into it. Did you know wigs were made out of dead people's hair? They waited till poor people died and then shaved their heads. I think costumes for that period should reflect how they lived. They should be real and gritty and nasty. It's not right if they're all cleaned up.

I loved playing Mrs Candour: 'How have you been this century?' – that's chronic, that opening line, it's the funniest line in the play for her. I'd pause for a second, before I said it, to get the full relish. What I made up about her, in my own mind, was that she wasn't the same class as the other ladies that she was allowed to visit. They wouldn't have entertained her normally. They accept her because they have a good laugh and she can bring better gossip than anybody else can. When I did it, I walked very badly, with my bum up. She'd worked so hard at the gossip, walking behind the coaches with the coachmen and letting them have a little feel of her bosom, to get the scandal from them – she'd literally worn herself out on those cobbled stones, rushing after people and listening to everybody.

Those women – Mrs Candour and Lady Wishfor't – they always rather fancy themselves as well. They think they're a cut above the average. The class thing with those characters is so important. It takes me a long time to form a character.

I make it up as I go along but once I've got it, it's always there.

Coming to theatre from variety, I almost had to audition for the *actors* to begin with. I'd just done a year at the Palladium which made them trust me even less. *The Killing of Sister George* was the first play I'd ever done. I liked the script. I thought 'Oh yes, I can do that.' Yet when I did the film and Robert Aldrich took me to Gateways, the club in Bramerton Street, Chelsea, I nearly had a fit. I said, 'If I'd been here before I did the play, I'd never have done it.' I didn't realize they held each other's bums and went to the gents' loo. What did they do in the gents' loo? And Archie, the chucker-out with all these tattoos on her arms! But she was lovely. They all were, although they frightened me a bit to begin with because I didn't know exactly what it would be like.

My mother was terribly funny. Somehow she got to know all those kind of things before I did because she used to look at some woman and say, 'I think that's a collar and tie job, Beeryl'. Collar and tie job! I'd never heard anything like it. I'd say, 'Do you think so, Mummy?' She'd say, 'Oh yes, and I think it's a "what if I am".' Defiant, you see.

We died the death on the tour of *Sister George*. We emptied every theatre. We even had trouble getting served in shops, almost. I said to Joan, my helper, 'I know this can't be a success because we don't do any business.' We did two pre-views – one for nurses, one for policemen. They didn't know what it was about because they were all women, the nurses – and the policemen were all men. So that meant nothing. Then came the opening night and the audience were in hysteria. I thought Eileen Atkins had taken her knickers off or something. I kept looking round at her to see if she was doing anything a bit different, but she wasn't. On the first night, it was booked out for about five months – it was a *tremendous* success.

We've remained great friends, Eileen and I, since those *Sister George* days. We were rehearsing it in Bristol one time, and Eileen and I went for a few drinks in the pub at lunchtime. I said, 'Can you dance, Eileen?' She said, 'Oh yes.' So I said, 'Why don't we go in and show them a little dance?' That's how the Laurel and Hardy routine got in because we did 'By the light, of the silvery moon'. We both knew all the steps.

I suppose some people might have shied away from *Sister George*, thinking of their careers. I didn't care. I just wanted to act. It was the press's fault. When I did a couple of revues in London at the Globe, quite a few of the papers called me, 'this comedy actress', and I thought, 'Yes, that's what I want to be'. I don't know how I saw myself before, but I wanted to know what I was about. I suppose I had thought of myself more as a comedienne. I knew I could act because I could upset people, even in those little things at the Watergate. I could always get laughs with straight lines. To do sad things is so *easy*. People are so sentimental. To do funny things is much more difficult.

The difficulty for me was in getting people to take me seriously. In something like *Spring Awakening*, everybody expected I was going to be funny. I had to use all my will-power to stop them from laughing. You really have to show them it's never going to be funny, it's going to be tragic.

In *Sister George*, I had to work against the text. If I played for sympathy in that part, I never got it. If I played almost against the sympathy, then I got it. That was the only way I found out, by doing it. The whole thing about me and acting is that I have no technique. I've only gained knowledge as I've gone along. I know really technical actors who say, 'Oh, it's a matinée, I'll do a technical performance this afternoon, I won't let it touch me', but I can't do that. I'm destroyed whether it's a matinée or whatever it is. I've only got *me* to work on. I'm totally defenceless.

At the end of *Sister George*, I was despondence itself. I did it for a year and five months on the stage and then I did seven months in New York. I got the Tony award there. I didn't get any acknowledgement for it in Britain but that didn't matter; I got great satisfaction from it. I always took my radio with me and at the end of the performance I played some music or found somebody talking on a programme, to get myself off the ground to get home. It's awful if it affects you like that but if you've got anything there, let them have it. You might go through your life and never be able to do anything like that. Anyway, it comes back to you, a million-fold.

One of the things I loved doing was the *St Trinians* film. It had such a wonderful cast – Joyce Grenfell, Alastair Sim, Irene Handl as the English Literature mistress, Renee Houston as the art mistress, Hermione Baddeley as the Geography mistress and pissed all the time. I was the Maths mistress who played golf with a monocle and straight hair, frightfully grand. We had such fun doing it. One day we had a fight with flour and the next day with soot.

It was just a romp, although there was a set framework to the script. That was the success of it. When we were unruly we were wildly unruly, such as when we were told to have a fight or to chase the girls, or blow things up in the laboratory, which I was always doing. It was a wonderful film to be in. The humour of it still seems to appeal to people. I don't know why. I'm not one for analysis. If it works, it works. You've got to have that original instinct for comedy and I learned it in all those years of variety and revue, because if you were standing there telling jokes, the only way you'd survive was by screwing your ear to the audience.

Entertaining Mr Sloane was my favourite film. The dialogue was so marvellous: 'I wonder if you'd mind taking your trousers off, Mr Sloane, I do hope you don't feel there's anything behind my request'; 'Till I was fifteen, I knew more about Africa than I did about my own body. That's why I'm so pliable'. Kath is full of such affectations. Unfortunately, I never met Joe Orton, although I met his brother and sister when I did the play at the Royal Court. I've seen all the other plays by Joe but I think *Sloane* is the best one. It's got the funniest dialogue. It's the snobbism I suppose.

People say things all the time and get them wrong like, 'We started off with kwiche renaine', or 'The Prince of Wales, he's the hire to the throne'. I seem to remember such things quite easily, although sometimes now I'll have to write them down if they're just too long to remember. I think it's a facility I have.

I've never been out of work except for maybe an odd week or two. I never had to worry whether I was attractive enough. That never came into it – even when I've been marrying somebody. I've been married twice. Everything was always perfect at home. I made sure the food was always there but *I* couldn't always be there. The people I married were not as successful as I got to be and in those days – it's very much changed now – men wanted to be absolutely the top dogs. They'd get jealous. They didn't like the thought that anybody might call them Mr Reid in error.

Now, it's 'So and so's not working so he's looking after the children this week', or 'I'm doing the cooking, he's doing the washing up'. That wouldn't have existed in my time. I was the dogsbody so I had to buy the food on the way to work, cook it when I got back and keep the house going. I was never kept by anybody. I was always the breadwinner, but I also had to play things down and pretend not to be quite so successful or very popular. It was hard.

It was even harder to be paying for everything. What did they want? For me to do well and be able to keep them in luxury: 'I want some new golf clubs'; 'Oh, all right' – and then they'd be cross because somebody made a fuss of me. It was an impossible situation. It wouldn't have happened if I'd been born slightly later.

It's not that I'm confident. I'm so easily squashed, you'd be amazed. I think I am resilient, more than anything. I refuse to be defeated by all the terrible things that have happened to me physically in the last three years. I can't walk down a staircase now, so if I'm working, I have to say, 'I'm sorry, I can't walk down it'. There are so many little things that irritate me about it. Sometimes my back is so painful I can't stand.

I still accept work. It's just that I have to assess it carefully beforehand to make sure I'm going to be able to do it well. I don't want to do anything badly. I don't want to lower my standards. It doesn't matter if I do a bit less as long as the standard is as high as I would like it to be.

It's tough that I can't rush off and do several things all in one day like I used to. That's what happens as one gets older. Small things suddenly become very important. I had my little stool out in the garden during the nice weather and I was pruning some roses and I thought, 'That's good'. That goes down under the heading of 'achievement'.

I've had marvellous health up until now. If I've had to have big operations, I've had them but, because of my insatiable desire to work and live, I've been up in a third of the time I should have been.

One of my criticisms of myself is that work has always come first. I've always gone back to jobs too soon. When I was doing *Gigi*, I was doing high kicks and splits and everything. That was only three years ago. I had an operation on my knee but went back to work long before I should have done and I was still on crutches. I'd put the crutches on the side of the stage and go on and do those numbers. I shouldn't have done. It's caused permanent damage to the knee. But if anybody had said that to me, I wouldn't have listened to them. I'd have said, 'Of course I can do it.' It's the old-fashioned thing, 'the show must go on'. That's rubbish because people take matinées off much more now. I've always thought, 'Oh god, if I'm off, they won't give me another job.' That's where the lack of confidence is. Every time a show finishes and I'm packing the makeup, I think I'll never get another job. The manic depression of finishing a show prevents you from thinking, 'I got a job before so I probably will get one again'.

I've done so many things and enjoyed so much. I'll keep on working just as long as anybody wants me.

Booklist

The following books, which were used in the preparation of this book, readers might also find of additional interest.

Wendy Chapkis, *Beauty Secrets* (The Women's Press, 1988)
Simon Callow, *Being an Actor* (Penguin, 1984)
John Berger, *Ways of Seeing* (BBC and Penguin, 1972)
Germaine Greer, *The Obstacle Race* (Secker & Warburg, 1979)
Carol Rutter, *Clamorous Voices* (The Women's Press, 1988)
Judith Cook, *Women in Shakespeare* (Harrap, 1980)
Lesley Ferris, *Acting Women* (Macmillan, 1990)
Sue Todd (ed.) *Women and Theatre, Calling the Shots*
    (Faber & Faber, 1984)